Rousseau and
The Social Contract

'Christopher Bertram leads the reader through Rousseau's *Social Contract* with clarity, care, and a fine sense of the work's underlying complexity. At each step of this most illuminating journey, Bertram takes the time to explore alternative meanings and make textual connections that deepen our understanding of Rousseau's political philosophy.'

Grace Roosevelt, *Metropolitan College of New York*

'This will prove to be a very useful and widely used commentary on the *Social Contract* filling a surprising gap in the market. It is sober, lucid and well-judged throughout and will, I am confident, be justly well-received, well-respected and well-thumbed.'

Nicholas Dent, *University of Birmingham*

Rousseau's *Social Contract* is a benchmark in political philosophy and has influenced moral and political thought since its publication.

Rousseau and The Social Contract introduces and assesses:

- Rousseau's life and the background of the *Social Contract*
- The ideas and arguments of the *Social Contract*
- Rousseau's continuing importance to politics and philosophy.

Rousseau and The Social Contract will be essential reading for all students of philosophy and politics, and anyone coming to Rousseau for the first time.

Christopher Bertram is Senior Lecturer in Philosophy at Bristol University.

IN THE SAME SERIES

Routledge Philosophy GuideBook to

Rousseau and
The Social Contract

Christopher
Bertram

 **Routledge**
Taylor & Francis Group

LONDON AND NEW YORK

First published 2004 by Routledge
11 New Fetter Lane, London EC4P 4EE

Simultaneously published in the USA and Canada
by Routledge
29 West 35th Street, New York, NY 10001

Routledge is an imprint of the Taylor & Francis Group

© 2004 Christopher Bertram

Typeset in Aldus and Scala by
Florence Production Ltd, Stoodleigh, Devon
Printed and bound in Great Britain by
TJ International Ltd, Padstow, Cornwall

British Library Cataloguing in Publication Data
A catalogue record for this book is available from
the British Library

Library of Congress Cataloging in Publication Data
Bertram, Christopher, 1958–
    Routledge philosophy guidebook to Rousseau and
    The social contract/Christopher Bertram.
        p. cm. – (Routledge philosophy guidebooks)
        Includes bibliographical references (p.) and index.
    1. Rousseau, Jean-Jacques, 1712–1778. Du contrat
social. I. Title: Rousseau and The social contract.
II. Title. III. Series.
JC179.R88B48 2003
320.1′1 – dc21   2003046655

ISBN 0–415–20198–5 (hbk)
ISBN 0–415–20199–3 (pbk)

Contents

REFERENCE KEY TO CITED
ROUSSEAU TEXTS

Oeuvres Complètes under the direction of Bernard Gagnebin and Marcel
Raymond (Paris: Pléiade, 1959–1995), five vols, cited in-text in the
form OC: volume number.

The Social Contract. All citations of the *Social Contract* are from Victor
Gourevitch ed. and trans. *The Social Contract and Other Later
Political Writings* (Cambridge: Cambridge University Press, 1977).
Reference is always given in-text in the form Book. Chapter.
Paragraph. So, for example, the first paragraph of Book 2, Chapter
7, 'Of the Lawgiver', would be given as 2.7.1.

Discourse on the Origins of Inequality, *Essay on the Origin of Languages*, and
Letter to Voltaire, are cited from Victor Gourevitch ed., *The Discourses
and Other Early Political Writings* (Cambridge: Cambridge University
Press, 1997) in the form G1: page number.

Discourse on Political Economy, the *Geneva Manuscript*, *Considerations on
the Government of Poland* and the *Letter to Usteri* are cited from
Victor Gourevitch ed., *The Social Contract and Other Later Political
Writings* in the form G2: page number.

Emile. References are to the standard translation by Allan Bloom (New
York: Basic Books, 1979) and take the form E(book number): page
number.

Correspondence. References are to the *Correspondance Complète*, ed. R. A. Leigh (Geneva and Oxford: Institut et Musée Voltaire and Voltaire Foundation, 1965–89) in the form CC, volume number, page number.

The Confessions, trans. J. M. Cohen (Harmondsworth: Penguin, 1953).

Reveries of the Solitary Walker, trans. P. France (Harmondsworth: Penguin, 1979).

Politics and the Arts: Letter to D'Alembert on the Theatre (ed. Allan Bloom) (New York: The Free Press, 1960).

The Collected Writings of Rousseau vol. 6: Julie or the New Heloise, edited and translated by Philip Steward and Jean Vaché (Hanover, NH: University Press of New England, 1997).

The Collected Writings of Rousseau vol. 7: Essay on the Origin of Languages and Writings Related to Music, edited and translated John T. Scott (Hanover, NH: University Press of New England, 1998).

C. W. Hendel ed. *Citizen of Geneva: Selections from the Letters of Jean-Jacques Rousseau* (New York: Oxford University Press, 1937).

John Hope Mason, *The Indispensable Rousseau* (London: Quartet, 1979).

The regiment of Saint-Gervais had done its exercises, and, according to the custom, they had supped by companies, most of those who formed them gathered after supper in the St. Gervais square and started dancing all together, officers and soldiers, around the fountain, to the basin of which the drummers, the fifers and the torch bearers had mounted. A dance of men, cheered by a long meal, would seem to present nothing very interesting to see; however, the harmony of five or six hundred men in uniform, holding one another by the hand and forming a long ribbon which wound around, serpent-like, in cadence and without confusion, with countless turns and returns, countless sorts of figured evolutions, the excellence of the tunes which animated them, the sound of drums, the glare of torches, a certain military pomp in the midst of pleasure, all of this created a very lively sensation that could not be experienced coldly. It was late; the women were all in bed; all of them got up. Soon the windows were full of female spectators who gave new zeal to the actors; they could no longer confine themselves to their windows and they came down; the wives came to their husbands, the servants brought wine; even the children, awakened by the noise, ran half-clothed amidst their fathers and mothers. The dance was suspended; now there were only embraces, laughs, healths and caresses. There resulted from all this a general emotion that I could not describe but which, in universal gaiety, is quite naturally felt in the midst of all that is dear to us. My father, embracing me, was seized with trembling which I think I still feel and share. 'Jean-Jacques,' he said to me, 'love your country. Do you see all these good Genevans? They are all friends; they are all brothers; joy and concord reign in their midst. You are a Genevan . . .'

The Letter to D'Alembert on the Theatre

INTRODUCTION

I first read Rousseau's *Social Contract* when I was about fifteen years old. The boyfriend of my French exchange partner's elder sister was interested in philosophy and he persuaded me to read a number of works of which Rousseau's was one. At the time, it was hard for me to distinguish Rousseau from Marx or Nietzsche since they all seemed to preach a message sharply at variance with the norms of English middle class society. Shortly afterwards, I acquired my own copy (and an edition of Hobbes's *Leviathan*) following the expulsion of their original owner from our public school.

In the thirty-odd years since, I have read the *Social Contract* and many of Rousseau's other works over and over again. The *Social Contract*, in particular, is an elusive text. It is somewhat fragmentary and poorly integrated. As a consequence, it has given rise to multiple and contradictory interpretations. To some of his readers, Rousseau has seemed to be the prophet of a participatory democracy; to others, he is the harbinger of twentieth-century totalitarianism. Some have seen the *Social Contract* as being apart from the main body of his work; others have found ways of integrating it with Rousseau's wider thought.

I cannot pretend here to have given anything like a definitive interpretation of Rousseau's text. There is, for good or ill, room for a multiplicity of Rousseaus.[1] But I have tried, throughout, to make his ideas plausible and attractive, insofar as that is possible. Certainly, I have endeavoured to resist the Cold War readings of Rousseau that saw him as advocating an enclosed and all-controlling society. By contrast, I have attended to the liberal and republican aspects of his thought and noted that many sentiments, arguments and statements that have been held up as evidence of his 'totalitarianism' are, in fact, shared with other thinkers – such as John Locke – who are remembered as paragons of liberty.

The fragmentary nature of the text makes for some difficult choices in a work of commentary. Unlike, say, Hobbes, Rousseau is not good at deploying systematic argument. His comments on the general will, for example, are interspersed through the text and the reader has to cope both with the experience of suddenly coming across a comment that appears radically to contradict what has been said a few pages before and, hence, with the task of making the various passages consistent with one another. Rousseau can also be highly repetitive, so, for example, we find that much of Book 2 Chapter 6 recapitulates material that has been stated only two chapters previously. There is also the difficult question of how far we let the text stand on its own, and how far we bring to bear the wider context of Rousseau's writings. On the whole, and at the risk of repetition, I have tried to stick to the order of the text with the thought that the reader may be following the *Social Contract* alongside this work. There is also a difficult choice about what to leave out. Some commentators deal with the whole of Rousseau's book, others stick to the core passages of Books 1 and 2 which have been the most philosophically influential. I have tried to comment on the whole text with the exception of Book 4, Chapters 3 to 7 which seem of little enduring interest even to the most committed Rousseau anorak. One writing decision which may jar with some readers is my use of the male pronoun throughout. I would defend this not only on grounds of euphony, but also because it reflects Rousseau's own regrettably sexist outlook: Rousseauian citizens are men.

As to the interpretive choices made in what is to follow, I should highlight two: first, I incline to construing the general will democratically, rather than counterfactually. By this I mean that I take seriously Rousseau's insistence that a legitimate state is one governed by the sovereign people according to their general will which is normally to be identified with decisions they actually take, so long as conditions are right. I therefore reject the idea that the general will corresponds to some ideal standard, at one or two removes from what the people actually think about it. But more will need to be said to clarify this point. Second, I place quite some weight on Rousseau's critique of Diderot from the unpublished second chapter of the *Geneva Manuscript* draft of the *Social Contract*: political institutions enable us to approximate – by artificial means – the rational nature that we cannot realise unaided. Again, more will need to be said.

Rousseau is an important figure in our intellectual heritage. At some times his stock is high, at others less so. He is liable to be feted or reviled as the ancestor and inspiration of child-centred learning, of hippie communitarianism, of green thinking, of radical democracy and so on. There is undoubtedly something right about this, but Rousseau usually resists attempts to pigeonhole him. If I were pressed to state a case for his enduring value, it would be this: Rousseau lived at a time when the application of scientific knowledge to social problems was seen as offering the possibility of transforming human life for the better. Rousseau was sceptical of this 'Enlightenment' project. That project is still with us today and similar bold claims are being made for it. But for Rousseau our deepest human needs consist in establishing a connection between ourselves and others which guarantees us our sense of ourselves as possessors of value. He himself ended his life with a sense of radical disconnection from the rest of the human race, but his insight that the very systems, the markets and hierarchies that enable us to achieve mastery over the natural world can at the same time combine to frustrate and isolate us, still retains its power.

In working on the *Social Contract*, I have often relied on two other commentators in particular. First, Hilail Gildin's *Rousseau's Social Contract: The Design of the Argument* is an indispensable guide for any Rousseau scholar. Second, I was lucky enough to find a copy of Maurice Halbwachs's edition/commentary of *Du Contrat Social* in a second-hand bookshop. Halbwachs, a great sociologist as well as a philosopher, who perished in a German concentration camp at the end of the Second World War, provides a detailed commentary on every chapter and had an encyclopaedic knowledge of the relation between Rousseau's text and those of his forbears and contemporaries.

I owe thanks to many people for their witting and unwitting assistance in this project. Pascal Lemaignan and Bruce Dickinson, though unknown to one another, accidentally conspired many years ago to get me reading Rousseau in the first place. Stuart MacNiven, Jon Mandle, Bob Stern and especially Jinx Roosevelt commented on drafts of parts of this book. Andrew Chitty offered some early bibliographical help. I bounced various ideas to Jimmy Doyle, and sometimes he bounced them back. Nicholas Dent was good enough to correspond with me from time to time, and also offered very useful comments on the penultimate draft, as did Jo Wolff. The participants in my Rousseau course at the University of Bristol often gave me much to think about and I shall remember them with affection. Philippe Van Parijs and the members of the Chaire Hoover at the Université Catholique de Louvain and Bernard Silverman and the staff of the Institute for Advanced Studies at the University of Bristol both gave me highly congenial environments in which to write, away from the distractions of the Bristol Philosophy Department. I should also thank Pauline, Alex and Nick for their love and support during the composition of this book.

NOTE

1   As Judith N. Shklar so wisely puts things, 'I have come to accept that he is one of those authors who says something personal to every reader, and that it is both vain and illiberal to insist that one's own reading is the only right one', *Men and Citizens*, p. vii.

1

ROUSSEAU, THE MAN

When we study the work of philosophers like Hobbes, Locke or Kant, we normally feel that we can do so without knowing much about their lives and personalities. Certainly, such facts can be interesting, but they are hardly essential to our understanding. Jean-Jacques Rousseau is hard to treat in the same detached fashion. He thought of his life and his work as a complete whole, and of his work as expressing a unique central principle, namely that man is naturally good and becomes evil only through society.[1] This commendable will to integrity can become a burden rather than an asset once the facts of his life and personality are known, since many of the facts that form the integral whole do not reflect well on him. Rousseau was an unstable and even paranoid individual for considerable periods of his life and despite promoting an ideal of authenticity and transparency in social relations has left us accounts of his life that sometimes cast doubt on his capacity for knowledge of himself. His psychological difficulties have also provided ammunition to a variety of hostile commentators who have sought to interpret his work in all areas as simply expressing his derangement. So it is important, from the outset, to have some conception of his life and work as a whole, of his own view of them and how they fit together.

Students of philosophy or political theory, who come to know Rousseau primarily through the *Discourse on Inequality* and the *Social Contract* are often surprised to learn of the breadth of his achievement. His treatise on education – *Emile* – made a lasting contribution to childcare and pedagogy. His novel *Julie or La Nouvelle Heloise* was one of the most popular novels of the century. In music he became famous both as the composer of the smash hit opera of the 1750s – *Le Devin du Village* ('The Village Soothsayer') – and as one of the chief protagonists in a cultural war between the upholders of the French operatic tradition and the devotees of the simpler Italian style. As a cultural critic he also famously opposed d'Alembert's proposal that a theatre should be erected in Geneva by contrasting the theatre – where passive spectators have their emotions manipulated by actors who do not feel the passions they simulate – with the idea of genuinely inclusive festivals of the people. Through these various writings and through his lifelong interest in botany he promoted a new attitude to and appreciation of the natural world. Finally, in his various autobiographical writings Rousseau tried to explore how he became who he became and reveals his pain at his inability to realise relationships that embody the values of directness, transparency and immediacy.

CONFESSIONS

Our first and primary source for Rousseau's life are these various attempts at autobiography. The most ambitious of these is the *Confessions*, but we also have a series of letters to the French censor Malesherbes, the paranoid but insightful *Dialogues*, and finally the wistful and beautifully written *Reveries of the Solitary Walker*. The *Confessions* purports to be 'a portrait in every way true to nature',[2] and aims to sketch an inner history that will explain how Rousseau became himself, shirking no detail however embarrassing and humiliating to their author. However bad things are, though, the Rousseau of the *Confessions* seems confident that he will emerge from the telling of his life with at least comparative credit when he says of his audience, 'Let them groan at my depravities, and blush for my misdeeds . . . and may any man who dares say, "I was a better man than he".'[3] Indeed, Rousseau's depiction of events, sometimes hilarious, sometimes tragic, is often remarkable for its frankness.

These moments of extreme candour contrast sharply with other episodes that betray an astonishing lack of self-knowledge. Rousseau often seems to have been genuinely mystified at the attitude that others took to him: why would they not endorse his own view of himself as uniquely committed to truth, honesty and friendship? He is quick to see others as being motivated by malice, is extremely suspicious of any generosity shown towards him, and increasingly sees so-called friends and associates as being implicated in a giant conspiracy against him. Although it is easy to see all this just as a manifestation of Rousseau's own psychological difficulties, a fair account will reveal that not all of the malice directed towards him was simply imagined. In Rousseau's case, Voltaire in particular seems not to have lived up to the maxim of tolerance sometimes attributed to him: 'I disapprove of what you say, but I will defend to the death your right to say it.'[4] And following the publication of *Emile* and of the *Social Contract* in 1762, Rousseau became the victim of persecution from the states of both France and Geneva and, partly as a result, the object of overt public hostility. Under these circumstances, it is hardly surprising that someone as sensitive as Rousseau undoubtedly was should manifest his personality in an extreme manner.

GENEVA

One of the central facts in understanding who Rousseau was – and who he believed himself to be – has to be his Genevan background. He was born in the city on 28 June 1712. The birth was a difficult one and his mother Suzanne, a member of the patrician Bernard family, only lived for eight days after the appearance of Jean-Jacques. This meant that his father, Isaac Rousseau, a watchmaker, was left to bring up the boy alone. Isaac, though a citizen, was far from wealthy and the increasingly impoverished family had to move to the artisan quarter of St Gervais, a centre of radical dissent. Eighteenth-century Geneva was a state that, like so many since, was torn between its sociological reality as a plutocratic oligarchy and a legitimating myth of freedom, equality and democratic inclusion. The theologian Calvin, in his role as lawgiver, had devised a constitution for the Protestant city-state in 1541 and had vested sovereignty in the body of citizens. But at least by Rousseau's day, this was just the surface form of things. Although the citizens were nominally sovereign, actual power was vested not in the *Conseil General* (their annual assembly) but in the smaller *Grand Conseil* (200 members) and the *Petit Conseil* (25 members). Since even the citizens represented a mere ten per cent of the population (the rest being non-citizen immigrants and their descendants), effective political power was, therefore, in the hands of a very narrow oligarchy indeed. The question of who had the right to rule was a matter of bitter contestation that sometimes became violent and bloody. This was a conflict not just about the rights and wrongs of democratic and oligarchic forms of government, but also the proper meaning and interpretation of Genevan identity.[5]

Rousseau's father brought him up to have a strong sense of patriotic identification and a sense of republican virtue fostered by father and son reading the classics, and especially Plutarch, together. The ideal of the ancient republic that Rousseau picked up from those readings was something that he eventually imported into his aspirations for his homeland. Rousseau marked his own attachment to the city by styling himself 'Citizen of Geneva', though this was not something he was entitled to do between his conversion to Catholicism in 1728 and his reconversion in 1754. His attitude to the city emerges most strikingly in two pieces of writing: the dedicatory essay to the *Discourse on Inequality* and the *Letter to D'Alembert* on the Theatre. Given Genevan reality, the praise Rousseau heaps on the city in the dedicatory essay cannot be taken at face value, but probably represents an ironic attack on the city's oligarchy.[6] Rousseau is depicting the state not as it is, but as he would like it to be. He commends the republic for its democratic characteristics:

the sovereign and the people could have only one and the same interest, so that all the motions of the machine might always tend only to the common happiness; since this is impossible unless the People and the Sovereign are the same person, it follows that I should have wished to be born under a democratic government wisely tempered.

(G1: 114–15/OC3: 112)

But even if the institutions of Genevan life failed to measure up to Rousseau's aspirations, he nevertheless saw in its people the material from which virtuous citizens could be made. Nowhere does this come out more vividly than in the *Letter to D'Alembert*, where Rousseau invokes the image of the St Gervais regiment eating and dancing together and remembers his father pointing to the scene and telling his son to remember the brotherhood of all Genevans.[7] This notion of Geneva – though not its reality – thus expressed for Rousseau a political ideal: the possibility of realising in the modern world a republic of virtue to rival the Greek polis and the Roman republic, an amalgam of order and spontaneity where individual citizens partake freely in a relationship of unity.

ADOLESCENCE

This childhood of Plutarch and republican festivity was not to last forever. Isaac Rousseau was forced into exile following a quarrel in which he was unwise enough to unsheathe his sword. As a result, the young Jean-Jacques was sent to live with a pastor named Lambercier at Bossey, outside the city. It was here that he experienced the delights of corporal punishment at the hands of the thirty-year-old Mlle Lambercier, a taste that would remain with him always. The Lambercier household was also the birthplace both of his acute sense of justice and of his *amour propre*. The first was born when he was falsely accused and punished for breaking the teeth of a comb. He recounts how he boiled with indignation at being blamed for something he had not done. His *amour propre* took flight when the young Rousseau and his cousin diverted a ditch which pastor Lambercier had dug to water a newly-planted walnut tree. When the pastor discovers the diversion he exclaimed 'an aqueduct! An aqueduct', leading Rousseau to glow with pride at his precocity as a civil engineer.[8]

This happy period in his life did not last. Rousseau had to earn his living and was apprenticed as an engraver to a brutal master. One night the sixteen-year-old found himself locked outside the city gates, and, rather than face more punishment he decided to set off into the world. In neighbouring Savoy he was adopted by the young estranged wife of a Swiss nobleman: the Catholic convert Francoise-Louise de la Tour, Baronne de Warens. Mme de Warens promptly sent him off to Turin to be instructed in the Catholic faith. It is there, working as a servant in a noble household, that he committed an act which caused him lifelong shame: he falsely denounced a servant-girl for the theft of a ribbon that he himself had stolen, thereby bringing disgrace and probably penury on an innocent person. It is an episode that he returns to again and again in his autobiographical writings. His experience of being in service left him with a strong dislike of subjection to the will of others and a corresponding love of freedom and independence.

Rousseau soon made his way back to Mme de Warens's house and became, briefly, her lover. Sometimes he represents his life with her as idyllic, especially when he looks back in the *Reveries*, written at the end of his life. But at other times he recognises that the relationship with a woman he refers to as 'maman' is hardly one between equals. Nevertheless, it continued to be a model for love and friendship: with Mme de Warens he felt 'peace of heart, calmness, serenity, security, confidence',[9] feelings which were largely absent from his other relationships. We get a sense of how deeply unsatisfactory even this relationship was from the fact that he had to imagine himself with someone else during sex in order to preserve for himself his ideal conception of who she was.

FROM VENICE TO VINCENNES

Mme de Warens soon tired of her protégé, at least as someone to share her bed with. In the years 1740 to 1749 the building blocks for his future career were assembled. He enjoyed a brief career as a tutor (where he met Condillac for the first time). He also worked extensively on music and in 1742 presented a *Project for a New Musical Notation* to the Academy of Sciences in Paris.[10] It is also during this period that Rousseau started to think about writing a study of political institutions. He travelled to Venice as secretary to the French ambassador there and observed at first hand the sclerotic government of the Venetian republic. His stay in Venice was not only fateful for his political development, his exposure to the delicious music of Venice also shaped his aesthetic views.

The Rousseau of the 1740s was not, yet, the man who is famous today. He mixed freely with Diderot and his collaborators on the *Encyclopedie* and became a member of the Paris literary scene that he was later to reject. At this period he also met the woman who became the mother of the five children he was to deposit at the foundling hospital – Therese Levasseur, an illiterate laundry maid. We shall never know exactly what turned the Rousseau of the salons into the Rousseau we know today but, by his own account, he had a radically transforming experience in 1749 when he was on his way to visit Diderot who had been imprisoned at Vincennes. Rousseau had a copy of the *Mercure de France* with him and was reading it as he walked along. The paper carried the notice of a literary competition set by the Academy of Dijon who wanted contestants to discuss whether the re-establishment of the arts and sciences had contributed to the purification of morals. The sight of this question had a dramatic effect on Jean-Jacques:

> If anything was ever like a sudden flash of inspiration it was the impulse that surged up in me as I read that. Suddenly, I felt my mind dazzled by a thousand lights; crowds of lively ideas presented themselves at once, with a force and confusion that threw me into an inexpressible trouble; I felt my head seized with a vertigo like that of intoxication. A violent palpitation oppressed me, made me gasp for breath, and being unable any longer to breathe as I walked, I let myself drop under one of the trees of the wayside.[11]

Rousseau later claimed that at that very moment he grasped the principle which he says underlies all his work, namely that 'man is naturally good, and it is through these [social] institutions alone that men become bad.'[12]

However seriously we are disposed to take his story of this epiphany, Rousseau thereafter launched himself into an uncompromising critique of modern civilisation and especially of the enlightenment goal of a social order based upon the application of science to human problems. The first manifestation of this project was the brilliant essay which became the *Discourse on the Arts and Sciences*. With this he succeeded in winning both the prize set by the Dijon Academy and a widespread notoriety. For a moment, Jean-Jacques enjoyed great success which he built on with works like his *Discourse on the Origins of Inequality* (another entry for a prize for the Dijon Academy, coming second this time) and contributions to Diderot's *Encyclopedie*. But it was not as a social theorist or as a philosopher that Rousseau was best known before 1762.

MUSIC

In fact, in the mid-1750s Rousseau was at least as famous as a musical thinker and composer. He was one of the protagonists of the 'Querelle des Bouffons', a bitter argument between the protagonists of French and Italian music that followed the visit to Paris in 1752 of an Italian company performing Pergolesi's *La Serva Padrona*. Rousseau had also been the principal contributor on musical topics to Diderot's *Encyclopedie*. In both of these roles, he had greatly antagonised the dominant figure in French music, Jean-Phillipe Rameau. Rameau had become celebrated for establishing music on a set of universal principles drawn from mathematics and the physical sciences through his *Treatise on Harmony* and other writings. Rousseau thought that this whole 'scientific' approach missed the *imitative* essence of music. Rousseau believed that music should aim at communicating and arousing the passions in the listener through an appropriately designed melody. This was not, typically, something that could be done without regard to the subjective, human situation of the listener. Rather, in doing its work, music relied on culturally specific associations. However, not all cultures were equally suited for this task.

Rousseau alienated the French operatic establishment by claiming that the French language was by its very nature unsuited for music. This cultural conflict – which some French conservatives have seen as an attempt by non-French subversives (such as the Genevan Rousseau and the German Grimm) to undermine the integrity of French culture (and pave the way for social and political upheaval)[13] – has a curious after-history in the incorporation of some of Diderot's reflections on the matter in Hegel's *Phenomenology of Spirit*.[14]

Popular acclaim, as opposed to elite antagonism, came Rousseau's way in 1752 when his opera, *Le Devin du Village* was performed. The king loved it, and according to Berlioz 'never tired of singing *J'ai perdu mon serviteur*, more out of tune than any of his subjects'.[15] History, as Berlioz also records, has not been so kind in its judgement on *Le Devin*. The opera is a confection of simple tunes sung by simple folk: shepherds and shepherdesses. In one sense it is a realisation of Rousseau's aesthetic views (the simple tunes) but its success must in part be down to the fact that he was able to write the songs in the inherently unmusical French. The opera stayed in the repertoire until the 1820s, but then disappeared.[16]

FICTION

Rousseau also extended his creative talents to fiction and, in 1761, he published *Julie or La Nouvelle Heloise*, an epistolary novel on the model of Richardson's *Clarissa*. Like *Le Devin* it too was a tremendous success. The novel depicts the tangled involvement of the heroine with the figure of St Preux and with her husband Wolmar. It was an opportunity for Rousseau to explore in fictional form many of the aesthetic and philosophical themes that he deals with more formally elsewhere. Contemporary readers were shocked at the novel's emotional intensity. (It is hard for modern readers of the text to get the same effect!) There were seventy-two editions in French by 1800 and the work was widely translated into other languages. David Hume considered it to be Rousseau's masterpiece.

CONDEMNATION

In retrospect, 1762 should be seen as the moment of Rousseau's greatest success, but it did not seem so at the time. That year saw the appearance of both *Emile* and The *Social Contract*. Each of them is a remarkable work and I shall have more to say about the arguments of each in due course. *Emile* is simultaneously a treatise on childcare and education, a work of psychology, an anticipation of Hegel's *Phenomenology*, and a novel! It contains some of Rousseau's deepest insights into the nature of the good life and also some of the views that bring most discredit on him – such as his extreme misogyny. The *Social Contract* is the culmination (and part abandonment) of the social contract tradition and a work that has set many of the terms of subsequent debate in political philosophy. But though such are the features of these works that most interest us today, it was their religious content that antagonised the Genevans and Parisians of the eighteenth century. The *Social Contract*'s last chapter on the 'civil religion' contained comments on the incompatibility of Christianity with civic virtue that many found offensive (though offending people was not Rousseau's intention) and *Emile* contained a long quasi-independent section called 'The Profession of Faith of the Savoyard Vicar' which cast doubt on familiar aspects of Christian doctrine such as original sin. Both works were condemned by the Genevan authorities, and the condemnation of *Emile* by the Paris Parlement led to Rousseau 's flight and exile. He sought protection first under Frederick II and his governor, the former Jacobite Marechal Keith in Switzerland. Later (in 1765) he travelled to England as the guest of David Hume. He soon fell out with Hume, however, believing the Scottish philosopher to be implicated in a plot against him. After a brief spell in Derbyshire – where the locals referred to Rousseau and Therese as Mr Ross Hall and Madame Zell[17] – he returned to France in 1767. His paranoia continued and even intensified, no doubt exacerbated by the fact that there were those like Voltaire and Mme d'Epinay who genuinely wished him ill. The low point may have been his attempt to place the manuscript of his *Dialogues: Rousseau, Judge of Jean-Jacques* on the altar at Notre Dame in 1776.

These last years of Rousseau's life during which he struggled to compose his various autobiographical writings are both appallingly tragic and sometimes, because of the absurdity of many of Rousseau's delusions, hilariously funny. Living as a music copyist he spent much time walking and botanising while always being worried about his health and his enemies. Despite the fact that poor Therese had stuck with him through everything, he begins the *Reveries* with the words: 'So now I am all alone in the world, with no brother, neighbour or friend, nor any company left me but my own.'[18] The position of solitude that Rousseau reaches in the *Reveries* represents the total collapse of his hopes for a satis-factory place in society.

Although the fall that is central to Rousseau's analysis in the *Discourse on Inequality* was one from a state that could not be regained, it seemed that there could be a going forward either indi-vidually (with *Emile*) or collectively (with the *Social Contract*). But by the end of his life Rousseau seems to have given up all hope of entering into relationships other than ones of deception and exploita-tion. He had once entertained a hope for the future, but so powerful had his enemies become that such a hope must be abandoned too.

The human race has entirely turned against him, drawn into the all-pervading Diderot–Grimm conspiracy, which turns out to be God's will. He receives striking confirmation of the universal conspiracy and a sign of the attitude he should henceforth have to himself and the world when he is badly injured by being knocked down by a Great Dane. Reports of his death begin to circulate and subscription is opened to publish his complete works: what better indication of the fact that his enemies are preparing to publish forgeries under his name to discredit him!

IN RETROSPECT

Despite the oddity of his life, Rousseau has remained at the fore-front of our culture for a quarter of a millennium and the effects of his work continue to be felt. His immediate impact was, first, on the Romantic movement and second, philosophically, via Kant and Fichte. He played a crucial role in launching a new aesthetic of 'nature' which manifested itself in the work of poets, painters and composers (among others). The battle between the notion of nature as something essentially good and a bleaker Hobbesian view is fought out to this day in many fields, including, crucially, ideas on education. Sometimes Rousseau is in fashion, at other times not, but he never quite goes away. In political philosophy the Rousseauian heritage is ever present whether via Rawls's theory of justice or in various theories of deliberative democracy. He is a thinker who, for good or bad, remains with us.

NOTES

1 For attempts to interpret this principle, see, especially, Melzer, *The Natural Goodness of Humanity* and Cohen, 'The Natural Goodness of Humanity'.

2 *The Confessions*, p. 17; OC1: 5. The other indispensable source is Maurice Cranston's three-volume biography of Rousseau.

3 Ibid.

4 For Voltaire's perfidy see Cranston, *The Solitary Self*, p. 102.

5 For a fascinating account of the Genevan background to Rousseau's philosophical and political development, see Rosenblatt, *Rousseau and Geneva*, ch. 1.

6 See Rosenblatt, *Rousseau and Geneva*, pp. 84–7.

7 *Politics and the Arts*, p. 135n; OC5: 123–4.

8 *The Confessions*, p. 33; OC1: 24.

9 Ibid., pp. 86–9; OC1: 84–7.

10 Although this proposal was rejected by the Academy and its shortcomings were exposed by Rameau it did have a certain success when a version was adopted by an influential school of musical education in the nineteenth century and is still occasionally employed in the Far East. See the Introduction to *The Collected Writings of Rousseau vol. 7*, p. xvi.

11 Letter to Malesherbes, 12 January 1762, from Hendel, *Citizen of Geneva*, p. 208; OC1: 1135.

12 Ibid.

13 See Paul, 'Music and Ideology', pp. 395–410.

14 For the details, see Wokler, 'The Enlightenment', p. 169.

15 Berlioz, *Memoirs*, p. 52.

16 Though it is now available on CD.

17 See Cranston, *The Solitary Self*, p. 169.

18 *Reveries of the Solitary Walker*, p. 27; OC1: 995.

2

HUMAN NATURE AND MORAL PSYCHOLOGY

The *Social Contract* is but one of Rousseau's essays in political philosophy, albeit the most important one. Its connection to Rousseau's
wider body of thought is sometimes clear on the surface, but at
other times the links are more subterranean. In this chapter I say
something about the psychology and philosophical anthropology
that lies behind the political philosophy. But before I do, it may be
helpful for the reader to have a very brief initial summary of the
'plot' of the *Social Contract*. The *Social Contract* is organised into
four books, though what we have is a fragment of a larger project
on political institutions. In the first of these books, Rousseau's intention is initially negative: he is concerned to rebut what he takes to
be false theories of the legitimate authority of the state. This makes
way, at the end of the first book, for a statement of his own contractarian theory of political association and his statement of the problem
to which a theory of political right must provide an answer: namely,
how to combine individual freedom with political authority. In the
second book, Rousseau concentrates on the nature of the sovereign
people, outlines his conception of the general will and of the law

that flows from it and addresses some problems of the initial formation of the state via the figure of the 'lawgiver'. The third book
concentrates on the mechanism for the application and enforcement
of the general will in particular cases: the government. Rousseau
outlines what he takes to be the correct relationship between sovereign and government and the ways in which this relationship will
almost inevitably go wrong and lead to the end of the body politic.
This theme is continued into the beginning of the fourth book, most
of which is devoted to a survey of Roman political institutions but
which concludes with an important chapter on civil religion.

Rousseau does little in the *Social Contract* itself by way of systematic exposition of the philosophical anthropology that lies behind it.
What we find instead, is that Rousseau's ideas on that subject intrude
into the text rather like the visible pieces of icebergs. So, for example,
there seems to be an implicit narrative or pseudochronology that
informs some of Rousseau's discussion, involving a state of nature
of some kind and a process of socialisation and foundation of the
state. These are topics that Rousseau treats with much more
explicitness in texts such as the *Discourse on Inequality*, the *Essay
on the Origin of Languages*, and in the *Geneva Manuscript* draft
for the *Social Contract* itself. Similarly, Rousseau has much to say
in *Emile* – his treatise on education – about the way in which
environment and institutions can shape or deform the psyche, that
we can draw on to understand the *Social Contract*. Accordingly,
the purpose of this chapter is to prepare the way for our engage-
ment with the text of the *Social Contract*, by saying something
about the view of human nature and human flourishing that
Rousseau explores elsewhere.

One way of introducing Rousseau's psychological views is to contrast them with a picture of human flourishing inspired by Hobbesian
or Humean theories of action and motivation. According to those
views our lives go well or badly to the extent to which we succeed
in satisfying the desires we happen to have, where there is no further
question we can sensibly ask about whether those desires are good
or bad, rational or irrational.[1] Rousseau rejects the idea that our
various desires are all of a piece. Rousseau's position is that there is
a crucial distinction to be drawn between our desires in relation to

the physical universe around us and our desires concerning other persons, and that any view that ignores or abstracts from that distinction will fail to understand an essential element of our human lives. In summary, the Rousseauian view holds that underlying the desires that we happen to have is a basic drive for self-preservation which finds expression not only in the desire to care for our physical needs but also in a regard for our standing among other persons like ourselves. This thought interacts with a second Rousseauian theme: we come into the world with the emotional and cognitive equipment necessary for us to lead happy and fulfilled lives, but that very equipment, if wrongly managed or developed, can lead us into paths of misery, frustration and mutual destructiveness.

Rousseau's own exposition of these views is usually embedded in narrative. The two best-known examples are his *Discourse on Inequality* and *Emile*. In the first of these, Rousseau sketches a reconstructed history of the human race in order to show, among other things, that certain aspects of the human personality that have been taken to be natural are nothing of the kind, and to explain how various forms of consciousness and self-consciousness come into being together with structures of inequality, oppression and domination. In *Emile*, Rousseau moves from considering the collective case to examining the individual one and describes the education of a young man and the ways in which he might be educated so as to flourish in a hostile social environment. Although Rousseau uses this narrative form to expose and develop his view of human psychology and the good, the stories he tells are not essential to his theory which can largely be set out independently of those vehicles. The purpose of this chapter is principally to make such an exposition of his psychological views and to clarify the claim that he often asserts to be his central unifying idea, namely, that man is good by nature but corrupted by society.

BASIC IDEAS

Rousseau believes that human beings are fundamentally self-interested. They are constructed so as to care for themselves and their own self-preservation above all. As he puts this in *Emile*:

> The source of our passions, the origin and the principle of all the
> others, the only one born with man and which never leaves him so
> long as he lives is self-love [*amour de soi-même*] – a primitive, innate
> passion, which is anterior to every other, and of which all others are
> in a sense only modifications.
>
> (E4: 212–13/OC4: 491)

Stated in this way, it may look as if there is no real difference
between Rousseau and an egoist such as Hobbes. However, Rousseau
argues that on a correct understanding of what that self-love is and
where it lies, human beings will *not* be led into endemic conflict
with their fellows since, on such a proper understanding, caring for
one's own well-being requires one to grant proper consideration to
the fundamental interests of others. However, when the problem is
put in this way, as suggesting a lack of proper *understanding*, it can
appear that Rousseau's diagnosis of the human situation will call
for the application of reason and enlightenment to problems caused
by our misapprehension of our true interests. That is both a true
and a highly misleading picture of his view. Like Aristotle before
him (and Kant after him) Rousseau believes that human beings have,
as it were, two natures. On the one hand we are mammals guided
by instinct to satisfy our needs, on the other we are rational creatures (indeed creatures made in the image of God). Many of our
problems occur because we are stuck mid-way between these two
natures. Considered as mere animals, we have been endowed by
nature with the instinctual apparatus necessary for our individual
and collective preservation; as purely rational creatures we could
also be guided by conscience and morality to live together in peace.
As creatures caught between these two poles, we find our animal
instincts distorted by a debased reason in such a way as to thwart
both individual and collective peace and happiness.

What, then, does our self-interest basically consist in? As men-
tioned above, Rousseau makes a fundamental categorial distinction
between two sorts of desire. In the first place we have desires
corresponding to those interests which we share with all other
sentient beings: we need adequate nutrition, warmth, shelter and
so on. In the satisfaction of those desires other human beings may,

contingently, help or hinder us. We may hunt together or gather firewood together or we may use resources gathered by others or pre-empt their using some resource or whatever. To this extent, other human beings form part of the furniture of the world in the same way that boulders, trees, dogs, tigers and sharks do. But *crucially* we do not experience our relationship with other human beings just as hindrances or helps to the achievement of our goals. Human beings are willing, desiring creatures and they care about the wants and desires and attitudes that one another have, most significantly, the wants and desires and attitudes that they have about one another's wants and desires and attitudes. And they have reactions to the wants, desires and attitudes of others that are themselves wants, desires and attitudes. Even when we encounter others in the mundane business of securing our physical needs we cannot escape attributing intentions to them and we often have attitudes towards those intentions: attitudes of jealousy, resentment, injustice, sympathy and so on.[2] But the crucial arena where our attitude toward others has most significance, concerns the value they place on us not as instruments for the satisfaction of some end they happen to have, but in ourselves. Are we loved and respected by others or hated and despised? And we have our own opinion of ourselves that hangs, to a greater or lesser extent, on the opinion held of us by others. To be sure, our own opinion of ourselves can be more or less resistant to the opinion of others but, for Rousseau, the best life would be one where we are loved and respected for good reason by others whose opinion we value.

ROUSSEAU'S VOCABULARY OF THE PASSIONS

It is time to introduce some of the technical vocabulary Rousseau uses in discussing these ideas. The most basic drive that he attributes to human beings is what he calls *amour de soi* (self-love or love of self). This consists in a drive to take care of our own needs: our basic wants and interests. It is clear that he believes this to be a passion which humans share to some extent with all creatures, and at its most basic level it is just the instinct to survive and to preserve oneself. Rousseau distinguishes between this passion and another one, which he calls *amour propre*, and which is often some-what misleadingly translated as pride or vanity. His exposition of the relationship between these two concepts can be confusing (and this may reflect different stages in the evolution of his own thought) so that sometimes he regards these two passions as categorially distinct from one another with *amour propre* sharply contrasted with *amour de soi* and with the former given a strongly negative connotation. It appears, in these contexts, that *amour de soi* is a benign passion leading us to care for our physical well-being whereas *amour propre* is a bundle of toxic reactive passions that lead us into conflict with one another by fostering feelings of arrogance, pride, vanity and resentment. Such an account is supported by Rousseau's Note XV to the *Discourse on Inequality*, where he writes:

> *Amour propre* and *amour de soi-même*, two very different passions in their nature and their effects, should not be confused. Self-love [*amour de soi-même*] is a natural sentiment which inclines every animal to attend to its self-preservation and which, guided in man by reason and modified by pity, produces humanity and virtue. *Amour propre* is only a relative sentiment, factitious, and born in society, which inclines every individual to set greater store by himself than by anyone else, inspires men with all the evils they do one another, and is the genuine source of honor.
>
> (G1: 218/OC3: 152)

However, this early picture can lead us to misunderstand Rousseau's more developed and considered view. First, we should notice that *amour de soi* has two different (though related) senses. First, it is the *drive* to care for oneself in the most general sense, such that any act of caring-for-self – whether in respect of our animal needs or our rational nature – is a manifestation of *amour de soi*. Rousseau also uses the term, though, to denote not just this broad genus of drives and passions but also a subspecies of it that is contrasted with *amour propre*. When *amour de soi* is used in this contrastive sense, it may connote a mode of care for oneself qua natural or physical being. We are not just physical, biological beings though, we are also moral or social creatures and as such we have needs and interests that are proper to our nature as beings in a social world with other such beings. *Amour propre* is one of the forms that *amour de soi* (in the generic sense) takes in such a world of social beings: it directs us to look after our standing or status in such a world. In much of Rousseau's work, *amour propre* is seen as the root of conflict and frustration, as indeed it often is. This is because he believes that this drive to secure status and standing in a social world with others will, given features of society that normally (though contingently) hold, lead us into various social and psychological pathologies. But he emphatically does not believe that this form of *amour propre* is the form that it inevitably takes; rather it is a drive that must be satisfied if social and moral creatures are to secure their well-being, and which *can* be satisfied provided the right circumstances are nourished and attended to.[3]

Amour propre is not the only modification of *amour de soi* that is relevant to our life together with our fellows. Rousseau also endows us with the capacity for *pitié* – the capacity to identify sympathetically with the pain and suffering of others. In some of his writings, Rousseau draws a sharp distinction between *amour de soi* and *pitié*, positing them both as mutually independent original passions which we share with animals. In the *Discourse on Inequality* he writes:

> ... meditating on the first and simplest operations of the human Soul, I believe I perceive in it two principles prior to reason, of which one interests us intensely in our well-being and our self-preservation, and the other inspires in us a natural repugnance to seeing any sentient Being, and especially any being like ourselves, perish and suffer.
>
> (G1: 127/OC3: 125–6)

But in Rousseau's more mature reflections he sees *pitié* as a development of *amour de soi*, as a projection of our own care for self onto the suffering other, forming the basis for a recognition that it, too, is a creature like ourselves endowed with feeling and a viewpoint on the world.[4] At its most basic level, though, *pitié* is a minimally reflective sentiment. In its manifestation it need not

express anything so explicit as the thought that the other is a creature like myself and that, consequently, its pain ought to be relieved;
rather it is an instinctual response to the fact of that suffering giving
rise to an immediate desire to relieve it. As such it is not a moral
sentiment at all, but rather a pre-moral drive that tends to secure
what Rousseau takes to be the goals of morality without the need
for moral reasoning as such. In order to survive together, we need
some sentiment which will moderate our self-interest in a way that
will be mutually beneficial. We can see *pitié* as a naturally occur-
ring modification of *amour de soi* that conduces to the goal of *amour
de soi* (our self-preservation) by modifying its pursuit.

Two other, related, aspects of Rousseau's view of human nature
now need mentioning: that human beings are *perfectible* and that
they have free will. The first of these is just the observation that
human beings are capable of learning and are changed by what they
learn. Humans can develop (and indeed transmit to one another)
new ways of doing things. These may be new techniques – how to
hunt better or to work metals – or new social practices. The passions
that we are subject to will take different forms depending on the
technology and culture that we encounter. Second, we are free;
we are not simply the prisoners of instinct but have the capacity to
deliberate on courses of action and to choose one path over another.
Because we are free we can be held responsible for our actions, a
necessary condition for the intelligibility of many of the attitudes
associated with *amour propre*.[5] Rousseau does not argue for the
proposition that we have free will, he takes it to be a belief that is
simply inescapable for us.

Finally, Rousseau argues for the importance of *conscience*.
Unfortunately, he nowhere gives a systematic account of the importance of this attribute of our mental lives – perhaps the closest he
comes is in the *Profession of Faith of the Savoyard Vicar* and in
the related *Lettres Morales*. Conscience is distinct from reason, but
is clearly a part of our nature as rational creatures. It is a moral
faculty, but is, for Rousseau much more than that since it is implicated in our appreciation of beauty in art and nature and in our
commitment to truth as a norm of discourse. Most generally, it is
a love for the well-orderedness of the world and a corresponding

distaste for its disordered state. While reason alone might inform us of what principles of justice and morality are, it is conscience that inclines us to love the good and the just and to hate injustice.

THE PROBLEM OF DEPENDENCE

These various elements – *amour de soi, amour propre, pitié, free will, perfectibility* and *conscience* – come together in Rousseau's account of the pathologies of modern life and in his strategies, both educational and political, for avoiding them. The central problem here is one of *dependence*: dependence on others. We live in a world in which we are dependent on others in two ways: first, and most prosaically, we are dependent on others through an extensive system of social co-operation: the division of labour. Here, Rousseau anticipates Karl Marx. The products that most of us consume on a daily basis are the result of activities including growing, harvesting, mining, manufacturing and transporting that involve many thousands, perhaps millions, of people. Hardly anyone can supply their physical needs through their own unaided efforts. This interdependence was much less marked in Rousseau's own day than it is now, but even peasant farmers would have relied upon specialist producers such as blacksmiths, wheelwrights and tanners. Second, we are dependent upon others for our sense of self-worth. (Here Rousseau anticipates Hegel.) Our *amour propre* leads us to seek confirmation of our standing in a world of other beings. We seek recognition of our value, and our self-valuing is highly vulnerable to the opinion others have of us and the way they treat us.

This problem of dependence also connects to a problem of competitiveness and relative position. If we want someone to grant us preferment in the bestowing of either standing in the social world or material resources, we may well find ourselves in competition with others who seek the same regard from them. There will, therefore, be a premium on the possession (or, crucially, the appearance of having) those attributes that will lead other people to grant us their favours. In Rousseau's account of the genesis of *amour propre* in the *Discourse on Inequality*, he gives a crucial role to singing and dancing and the way in which comparative prowess in these activities might commend one to a sexual partner, the next step being jealousy and possibly murder. In *Emile* he writes: 'To be loved one has to make oneself lovable. To be preferred, one has to make oneself more lovable than another, more lovable than every other, at least in the eyes of the beloved object' (OC3: 494/E4: 214).

But in appearing as we believe another wants us to appear we run two risks: first if we do in fact change to conform to our perception of how another wants us to be we risk that our own self becomes somehow deformed or inauthentic; second, insofar as what we present to the other remains mere appearance, the recognition we secure from them is based on a mistake on their part that we know to be a mistake and so is devalued in our own eyes. Correspondingly, if we come to believe that the other person appears to us not as they are but as they believe we would like them to be, we may again become anxious about the authenticity of the relationship.

If relationships with friends and lovers are problematic, so are relations between those who can grant status or supply a service and those who want what they can offer. In a hierarchy, such as a state, or a political party or a firm, subordinates will seek the approval of their superiors in order to 'climb the greasy pole'. Here again there is a relationship of need and dependency, the subordinate needing the superior in order to gain resources or preferment, the superior needing the subordinate to carry out his will and to confirm his superior status. The recognition granted to the superior by the subordinate may well not be a genuine expression of admiration, though, but a response conditioned by cynical calculation, and the superior will often know or suspect that this is so. Accordingly, the recognition given by the subordinate will fail to satisfy the superior's *amour propre*. In some cases, superiors use their power directly to compel those subject to them to acknowledge their worth. They can sometimes succeed in eliciting this performance, as when the press magnate Robert Maxwell had his newspapers carry articles praising him or when the Romanian dictator Nicolae Ceausescu had crowds display his image and chant his name. For anyone not completely lacking in imagination, such forced recognition must be almost without value; when power depends upon it it is fragile. Ceausescu depended for his power on the willingness of his subjects publicly to proclaim his excellence, when some dared not to and others took up the call, his regime collapsed.

While Rousseau is most scathing about the distorting play of simulated recognition that goes on within hierarchies, it is clear that he thinks a similar process is at work in market relationships. Here, too, the relationship is not one between persons who genuinely recognise the worth of others, but between buyers and sellers whose interest in one another is purely instrumental. Sellers have an interest in representing their product as being more attractive than it really is – perhaps an interest in stimulating false needs – buyers must conceal as best they can their neediness in order to strike the most advantageous bargain. And each person harbours secret desires to profit from the misfortune of others. In the *Discourse on Inequality*, Rousseau is opposed to thinkers like Mandeville who believe that trade has a civilising effect on people:[6]

> I am told that Society is so constituted that every man gains by serving the rest; I shall reply that that would be all very well if he did not gain even more by harming them. There is no profit, however legitimate, that is not exceeded by the profit to be made illegitimately, and the wrong done a neighbour is always more lucrative than any services.
>
> (G1: 198/OC3: 203)

If Rousseau anticipates Hegel's discussion of lordship and bondage when he depicts hierarchical relationships, here he anticipates some of the young Marx's discussion of the exchange relationship.

These remarks may give the impression that Rousseau's depiction of human society as a manipulative contest of wills is limited to relations conducted within some contingently existing institutions: markets and hierarchies. But in fact Rousseau seems to think, at least once humans are fully human, that the risk of such manipulation is latent in human relations as such. In *Emile*, for example, he provides an analysis of the meaning of a baby's tears.[7] If the infant is responded to in the wrong way it will acquire a mental model of human relationships as being ones of domination, command and control, will consider itself entitled to command the wills of others and will experience resentment and fury if others do not conform to that will. Rousseau's programme of education is designed to head off this development so that the child does not develop a model of the social world as a contest of wills until it has reached a level of maturity such that these considerations can take their properly limited place in the child's mental life and conception of its own person.

In his most nightmarish representations of modern life Rousseau sees people entirely dominated by a world of opinion. In the *Discourse on Inequality* he contrasts the mental life of a European Statesman with that of a Carib (that is, a native inhabitant of the Caribbean):

> How many cruel deaths would not this indolent Savage prefer to the horror of such a life, which is often not even sweetened by the pleasure of doing well? But in order to see the purpose of so many cares, these words, *power*, and *reputation*, would have to have some meaning in his mind; he would have to learn that there is a sort of men who count how they are looked on by the rest of the universe for something, who can be happy and satisfied with themselves on the testimony of others rather than on their own. This, indeed, is the genuine cause of all these differences: the Savage lives within himself; sociable man, always outside himself, is capable of living only in the opinion of others and, so to speak, derives the sentiment of his own existence solely from their judgement.
>
> (G1: 187/OC3: 192–3)

This negative assessment of *amour propre* is elsewhere balanced by other thoughts. A few pages earlier in the *Discourse on Inequality* he had written:

> . . . it is to this ardor to be talked about, to this frenzy to achieve distinction which almost always keeps us outside ourselves, that we owe what is best and what is worst among men, our virtues and our vices, our Sciences and our errors, our Conquerors and our Philosophers, that is to say a multitude of bad things for a small number of good things.
>
> (G1: 184/OC3: 189)

Amour propre is, of course, not the only passion mediating our relationships with other persons. Pity also, crucially, plays a role. This role is partly epistemic: through our identification with the suffering of another person we acquire both a sense of our own human vulnerability and a recognition of our common humanity with them. We come to see that they are human as we are and we imagine ourselves in their place. This identification provides an instinctual basis for human beings to act in ways which are not in themselves moral – since the rightness of the action is not part of the actor's reason for performing it – but which functionally substitute for moral conduct. Given the imperfection of our nature, this instinct is often a surer guide to conduct than self-conscious moral reasoning which Rousseau thinks is often just a sophisticated rationalisation for self-interest. So, for example, in the *Discourse on Inequality*, Rousseau is scathing about philosophers who use their powers of reasoning to exempt themselves from helping their fellow human beings, whereas the untutored women of the street are led by their lively feelings of pity to restrain a fight. In the corrupt moral world even pity can be deformed in its function, though. Although it opens us to the suffering of the other, it is also a pleasurable sensation which gives those who experience it a sense of exception and escape from those very sufferings. Central to Rousseau's critique of the modern theatre in his *Letter to D'Alembert* is his noticing the way in which dramatic performance enables people to indulge the sweet sensation of pity and thereby to give themselves a certain opinion of their own moral worth.

It is not always easy to assign a particular feeling or sentiment to one of the underlying passions (*amour de soi*, *amour propre*, or *pitié*). One example of a sentiment with a mixed basis is patriotism. Patriotism has a rational basis in that citizenship and membership of the *patrie* gives individuals a security of equal standing with others, and thus satisfies their (non-inflamed) *amour propre*. But there are also elements both of *pitié* and of comparative pride in patriotism. So, for example, when Rousseau depicts the scene of the dancing regiment in his *Letter to D'Alembert*, the image we have is one of unreflective unity – oneness – with others. As we sing and dance together in a patriotic festival it may seem as if the very boundary between persons is blurred.[8] This oneness, this feeling of unity with the other is elsewhere identified by Rousseau with *pitié*. At the same time, our feeling of unity and togetherness with our fellow citizens – our fellow Genevans – is partly dependent on sentiments of pride that we are members of *this* group and not of another. Patriotism will also characteristically involve feelings of mild contempt towards those not lucky enough to be among the chosen people. Rousseau may or may not feel that this is rationally justified, but it does seem to form part of the psychological glue that keeps a people together.

THE NATURAL GOODNESS OF HUMANITY

Rousseau asserts in many of his writings that human beings are good by nature and are made wicked only in society. This claim has puzzled and infuriated readers and commentators from Rousseau's day to our own and has given rise to a variety of interpretations. In order to understand it, first we have to clear our minds of a modern, scientifically-influenced, conception of nature. In the modern, post-Darwinian view, nature is just what happens. With respect to biological organisms, such as plants or animals, a given genotype might achieve a variety of different phenotypical expressions, but we cannot say of one of those expressions that it is more natural than another. The same plant, for example, may appear larger or smaller or may bear flowers of one colour or another, or may be annual or perennial, depending on whether the climate is harsh or mild or whether the soil is acid or alkaline. On a premodern view of nature, influenced by Aristotle, by contrast, the nature of each organism consists in its striving towards a particular pattern or *telos*, the good of that organism is its achievement of that *telos* and its constitutive features and component parts are directed towards that end.[9]

Given this picture of nature, the claim that human beings are good by nature starts to look as if it might not be so much outrageous as platitudinous. All it would mean is that human beings are constituted in such a way as to realise a normal path of development for humans and that their component parts (including their *psychological* component parts) are designed for, and explained by, their fitness for that purpose. But difficulties arise once we realise that man has not one but *two* natures: an animal nature and a rational nature. This, at any rate, is what I take from passages such as this one, from the *Letter to De Beaumont*:

> Man is not a simple being; he is made up of two elements ... Self-love (*amour de soi*) is not a simple passion, but has two principles, namely, the intelligent being and the sensitive being, whose well-being is not the same. The appetite of the senses tends to that of the body and the love of order to that of the soul. This second love, when developed and made active, is called conscience; but conscience is only developed and only acts from enlightenment.[10]

Our animal nature is wholly good in that it directs us to our self-preservation instinctually and regulates conflict between individuals by the reflex of *pitié*. Our nature as free and rational beings is also wholly good in that it enables us to discover, through reason, sure principles of conduct and inclines us through conscience to obey them. But although society makes the realisation of our rational nature possible, it more often has the effect of undermining those features of our natural constitution that make for individual and collective good while failing to transform us completely into rational creatures. We are thus torn between our two natures, neither one thing nor the other, corrupted but not reconstituted; and the faculty of reasoning becomes an instrument of our debased passions rather than the expression of our autonomous nature.

The thesis of natural goodness is of crucial *political* importance for Rousseau. While he makes us aware of the world's injustice and oppression, its domination and slavery, he is also keen to empha-sise that these are the products of *contingent* features of our human nature. According to him we are not, to use the modern expression, *hard-wired* for aggression and domination; we have the possibility of creating and sustaining institutions of co-operation and social justice and of behaving decently and morally in our dealings with our fellow humans. Social corruption is very deep, however. Karl Marx once wrote that 'Men make their own history, but ... not under circumstances they themselves have chosen'.[11] Individuals and, indeed, peoples, encounter a world where human beings are already enmeshed in relationships that are corrosive both of their natural sympathy for one another and of their capacity for moral action. Only frameworks and strategies of an artificial nature can secure our escape. At the beginning of *Emile* Rousseau tells us: 'Everything is good as it leaves the hands of the Author of things; everything degenerates in the hands of man'. But after appearing to condemn the artificiality of human existence he writes:

> . . . our species does not admit of being formed halfway. In the present state of things a man abandoned to himself in the midst of other men from birth would be the most disfigured of all. Prejudices, authority, necessity, example, all the social institutions in which we find ourselves submerged would stifle nature in him and put nothing in its place. Nature there would be like a shrub that chance had caused to be born in the middle of a path and that the passers-by soon cause to perish by bumping into it from all sides and bending it in every direction.
>
> (E1: 37/OC4: 245)

THE ROLE OF ARTIFICE

If Rousseau is rightly interpreted as seeing our modern condition as being that of beings who are situated between a purely animal nature and a rational one, and who have, in a sense, developed some features of each of these personas at the expense of the whole, what is to be done? Rousseau's strategy in both *Emile* and the *Social Contract* is to develop artificial environments which enable us to approximate our rational nature given our foreseeable human limitations. Voltaire's maxim, 'the best is the enemy of the good', might, though, be applied with some justice to Rousseau's approach here. In our human world, a world of vice and competitiveness, the attempt to realise our semi-divine rational nature directly, and without protective and remedial artifice is doomed to failure.

In a world where *amour propre* has become a pervasive feature of our lives, the danger is always that the voice of nature either in the form of pity or of conscience will be silenced or smothered by our inflamed passions. In *Emile*, Rousseau pursues a programme of education that is managed in such a way as to avoid the premature birth of *amour propre* and to temper its emergence by providing the pupil with a more balanced estimation of his place in the world. In the *Social Contract* Rousseau aims, by means of a framework of institutions, to force citizens into a mode of thinking about themselves and others that imitates the mode of thinking required by their rational natures. The enjoyment of the status of equal citizen with others helps to satisfy the demands of *amour propre* and enables citizens to be governed according to a law they have given to themselves. But there is never a perfect fit between moral requirements of our rational nature and the requirements of citizenship. Our rational nature taken by itself would command us to obey the 'general will of the human race' – something close to the Kantian categorical imperative – but persons who would unconditionally abide by those requirements would deliver themselves to evil and destruction in a Hobbesian world.

Accordingly, or so I shall argue, the figure of the citizen, and the general will of the particular society of which he is a citizen, does not amount to a full realisation of our rational natures, but is rather a best approximation of it given man's fallen condition and limited reason. As we shall see, Rousseau got into a great deal of trouble for his assertion that a society of Christians would not sustain a vital republic. The *Social Contract* is not written on the assumption of moral perfection, but rather in the recognition that our *amour propre*, once awakened, needs careful management if it is not to destroy us.[12]

WAS ROUSSEAU RIGHT?

It may seem perverse to ask whether Rousseau is right or wrong about human nature. After all, we are reading an eighteenth-century thinker and from 250 years away, conclusions reached on the basis of a very different scientific and metaphysical framework from our own may seem to be of little use. Nonetheless, Rousseau's philosophical anthropology is at the service of an emancipatory political project and there is no shortage of writers today asserting something like the contrary of the natural goodness thesis and seeking to draw political conclusions from it. In a recent book on international politics, for example, the commentator Robert B. Kaplan explicitly endorses a Hobbesian view of human beings according to which 'altruism is unnatural, human beings are rapacious, the struggle of every man against every other is the natural condition of humanity, and reason is usually impotent against passion.'[13] It was views such as this one (among others) that Rousseau was concerned to reject in both the *Discourse on Inequality* and in *Emile*. Not that he doubted the observations on which such judgements are based: 'Men are wicked; a sad and constant experience makes proof unnecessary' (G1: 197/OC3: 202). But while such wickedness was found everywhere, Rousseau continued to affirm an original goodness that would make just social institutions more than an idle fantasy.

What does contemporary work in anthropology and primatology have to say about the dispute between Hobbes and Rousseau? First, Rousseau does seem emphatically wrong about one thing. In the *Discourse on Inequality*, he refuses the description of human beings as innately social animals. In his speculative reconstruction of history, our remotest ancestors are depicted as solitary creatures who wander through the woods and whose only interaction with other members of their species after early infancy is when they pause to copulate with a member of the opposite sex. In Note X to the *Discourse*, Rousseau speculates about whether or not 'orang-utans' are human. Remarkably, despite the fact that the animals Rousseau was designating by the term were almost certainly chimpanzees, Rousseau's account of early humans is not a bad approximation of orang-utan behaviour.[14] But orang-utans are actually atypical of the great apes (and of primates in general). The extensive and sophisticated social behaviour of gorillas, chimpanzees and bonobos is strong evidence that the most recent common ancestor that we share with those species was also social.

Not only are such species *social*, but they are also very hierarchical, with alpha-males dominating rivals by force and getting far more access to females than their subordinates. If hierarchy and domination as well as sociability are encoded in our human nature that is very bad news indeed for a political project such as Rousseau's. Fortunately for the hopes of such a project, though, primitive human groups do not exhibit the hierarchical structure typical of the great apes. Pre-state humans usually live in egalitarian social bands where leadership is a function of perceived expertise and where leaders who are perceived to rank themselves above their fellows risk ostracism or even death. Human societies do, though, exhibit a wider range of social forms than do any other primate species. Some human societies are extremely hierarchical (feudalisms, slave societies and Oriental despotisms come to mind), primitive bands are highly egalitarian, and modern liberal democratic societies combine equality of legal status with varying degrees of wealth inequality and, indeed, have social mores of varying egalitarianism. In his book *Hierarchy in the Forest*, Christopher Boehm, drawing on the work of Rousseau scholar Roger D. Masters, argues that humans have an ambivalent nature, one that makes both egalitarian and hierarchical social arrangements possible.[15] This distinguishes us from our primate ancestors whose genetic coding determined their hierarchical social structure. By contrast, human beings, once they had developed language and weaponry were able to enforce egalitarian social arrangements on would-be dominant members of their groups. The weak were able to subdue the strong in a Nietzschean reversal of the hitherto natural order that Boehm calls a 'reverse dominance hierarchy'. These egalitarian hunter-gatherer bands enjoy social and political arrangements that bear a striking resemblance to the ones Rousseau favoured: leaders exist, but are constrained to implement the general will of the group as a whole and disparities of wealth and status are kept to a minimum.

We should not get too carried away by the idyllic nature of these egalitarian bands. The freedom and equality that was characteristic of them was freedom and equality for men: women were socially subordinate. Nor were such groups havens of altruistic behaviour: a strong propensity to co-operate and share resources within a group was compatible with extreme cruelty and murderous intent towards members of other bands. Nevertheless, the compatibility of human nature with both hierarchical and non-hierarchical forms of social organisation at least makes an egalitarian and democratic political order such as Rousseau favoured a possibility that our human nature may not foreclose. In that sense, we might reinterpret Rousseau's slogan about the natural goodness of humanity. It is not that our human nature predisposes us to altruism and co-operation, but that it leaves open the possibility of more altruistic and co-operative social relations. Human beings may contingently be cruel and oppressive, but there is nothing in our nature that determines that things have to be that way and therefore necessitates the restraint of a *Leviathan* state.

THE PSEUDOCHRONOLOGY OF THE *DISCOURSE ON INEQUALITY*

In this chapter I have sought to present Rousseau's philosophical anthropology independently from the various narratives that he embeds it in. Nevertheless, it is useful for an understanding of what is to follow to know the outline of the story of human development that emerges from the *Discourse on Inequality*. In the second *Discourse*, Rousseau distinguishes four stages of development prior to civil society proper. In the first of these, solitary, wood-wandering creatures motivated by self-love and pity meet only rarely and accidentally. They have little or no sense that they might exist in the eyes of others. They are neither naturally sociable creatures, nor are they naturally hostile to one another. Rousseau describes them thus:

> . . . wandering in the forests without industry, without speech, without settled abode, without war and without tie, without any need of others of his kind and without any desire to harm them, perhaps without ever recognizing any one of them individually, subject to few passions and self-sufficient, Savage man had only the sentiments and the enlightenment suited to this state, that he sensed only his true needs, looked only at what he believed it to be in his interests to see, and that his intelligence made no more progress than his vanity.
>
> (G1: 157/OC3: 160)

But humans do not remain forever in this primitive state. The press of population increase gradually draws these creatures into more frequent interaction with one another, leading to a second stage where they start to develop some technical skills and the capacity to co-operate with one another. The representative image of this second phase is provided by Rousseau's account of a deer hunt. Individuals can perceive a common interest in co-operating together to catch a deer, but they have no real sense of belonging to a group as such and certainly no loyalty to one. If a tasty rabbit should come hopping past then individuals opportunistically desert their posts in order to satisfy their hunger. This phase eventually gives way to the 'golden age'. There are settled communities in which people first start to value themselves as others see them. *Amour propre* is born, but despite a growth in pride, vanity and even murder inspired by sexual jealousy, this stage represents a happy mean between the isolation of the original creatures and the total interdependence of 'civilised society'. Technical progress and, in particular the development of metallurgy and agriculture create an interest in distinguishing 'mine and thine' and this leads to the institution of private property and, eventually, inequality in holdings. The individuals of this final pre-political stage, inflamed by *amour propre* and divided into rich and poor are very close to the condition that Hobbes describes in Chapter 13 of *Leviathan*. A generalised civil war eventually leads the rich to propose the institution of government for mutual benefit. But, for Rousseau this 'social contract' is mainly a fraud perpetrated by the rich on the poor. The rich have succeeded in permanently freezing an unequal division of goods and of usurping the common force of society to protect their plunder and, thereby, stabilise social relations in their favour. The social state that issues from this agreement gives free play to inflamed *amour propre* and fails to realise the human needs even of those who are wealthy and who dominate the social hierarchy.

The conjectural history of the *Discourse on Inequality*, therefore, contains Rousseau's radical critique of modern society. One way of understanding the *Social Contract* is as sketching an alternative to the false equality represented by the social contract of the *Discourse*. It is to this that we now turn.

NOTES

1 For a modern exposition of a broadly Humean position, see Smith, *The Moral Problem*.

2 This play of intentions and attribution of mental attitudes is, of course, a staple of both modern philosophies of mind and language (such as H. P. Grice's theory of meaning) and of any number of country and western lyrics.

3 Here, especially, and elsewhere in this chapter I draw on, and am influenced by, Dent's pathbreaking *Rousseau*.

4 See, especially, the extraordinary discussion in Book 4 of *Emile* at E4: 221ff/OC3: 503ff.

5 A point famously made in recent philosophy by Strawson, in 'Freedom and Resentment'.

6 For a compelling discussion of Rousseau's relationship to the theorists of *doux commerce* see Rosenblatt, *Rousseau and Geneva*, pp. 76–84.

7 E1: 65–6/OC4: 286–7. See, especially, the discussion by Dent in *Rousseau*, pp. 70–4.

8 For a fascinating historical and psychological study of how dance can have this effect see McNeill *Keeping Together in Time*.

9 For a perspicuous contrast between the Darwinian and Aristotelian views, see Sober, *The Nature of Selection*, pp. 157ff.

10 OC4: 936. Translation in Hope Mason, *The Indispensable Rousseau*, p. 333.

11 Marx, 'The Eighteenth Brumaire of Louis Bonaparte', p. 146.

12 I have been somewhat influenced here by Scott's essay, 'Politics as the Imitation of the Divine', pp. 473–501, except that, crucially, Scott and I differ as to what the imitation of the divine involves.

13 Kaplan, *Warrior Politics*, p. 81.

14 For discussion of this note see, especially, Wokler, 'Perfectible apes in decadent cultures', pp. 107–34.

15 Boehm, *Hierarchy in the Forest*. See also Masters, *The Nature of Politics*.

3

MAN IS BORN FREE

(Book 1, Chs 1–2)

THE TEXT

Rousseau's treatise on political institutions bears the title *Of the Social Contract* or *Principles of Political Right*. The title suggests that we are being invited to a discussion of the basic organising principles of a political association or community. But Rousseau hesitated over the title and changed his mind several times before settling on his final choice. In the draft version – known as the *Geneva Manuscript* – we find *Of the Social Contract* crossed out, replaced with *Of Civil Society* and then reinstated. The subtitle there is first given as *Essay on the Constitution of the State*, replaced by *Essay on the Formation of the Body Politic*, replaced by *Essay on the Formation of the State*, which he in turn rejected in favour of *Essay on the Form of the Republic*. It is not clear that much depends on these equivocations, but they do presage a difficulty in classifying the text. Is Rousseau's foremost intention to write a treatise about constitutional law, political philosophy or political sociology?

Rousseau tells us that the work we have before us is just a fragment of a much larger one that he intended to write, a project he had first considered when he was secretary to the French ambassador to Venice in 1743. We cannot be sure what that book would have looked like had it been completed. It is clear, though from the single paragraph final chapter of the *Social Contract* (4.9) that the more extended work would have included considerable discussion on international relations as well as on the topics Rousseau ended up covering. After Venice, Rousseau seems to have returned to the idea of the project in spring 1756 at the Ermitage at Montmorency. But after the success of *La Nouvelle Heloise* in 1761 he came to realise that the project would take several more years to complete and decided that only a shorter work was within his powers.

We can see the basic ideas for the book surfacing in a number of places from about 1753. In the *Discourse on Inequality*, for instance, the dedication to the republic of Geneva anticipates some of the *Social Contract*'s key doctrines and the *Discourse on Political Economy* – an entry for Diderot's *Encyclopédie* – embodies Rousseau's central idea that a legitimate state should be regulated according to the general will.

Rousseau announces himself on the title page: 'by Jean-Jacques Rousseau, Citizen of Geneva' – proudly stating his affiliation with the state of his birth. Nor is Geneva the only city state invoked on that page. He adds an epigram: 'Foederis aeqas, dicamus leges'. 'Let us make equitable treaty terms' suggests King Latinus to his Trojan adversaries in Book XI of Virgil's *Aeneid*. King Latinus's hopes for peace were in vain, but Rousseau signals by his reference to the founding myth of Rome the classical stimulus for his own work. Venice, Geneva, Rome. Three republics, three sources for Rousseau's political thought. Not the only ones, to be sure. The *Social Contract* also contains many references (direct or indirect) to Sparta and to its founder Lycurgus.

In addition to the published text of the *Social Contract*, we also have a draft version. This text, known as the *Geneva Manuscript* is very close in content to the first two books of the final version, although certain differences are noteworthy. The single most significant divergence between the two texts is a chapter entitled 'On the

General Society of the Human Race' which Rousseau removed from the final version. We shall come to the question of that chapter presently.

MEN AS THEY ARE – LAWS AS THEY COULD BE

Rousseau's text proper begins with three paragraphs immediately preceding chapter one. These lines contain a striking series of contrasts. Rousseau tells us that he wishes to inquire whether in the civil order there can be a 'rule of administration' that is 'legitimate and sure' taking 'men as they are and laws as they could be'.[1] He tells us that he aims at an alliance of what 'right permits' with what 'interest prescribes' in order that justice and utility should on no account be opposed to one another. He announces then, from the start, that his project has an anti-utopian character. His contrast between 'men as they are and laws as they could be' echoes passages in Machiavelli, Vico and Spinoza, especially a comment at the beginning of the *Political Treatise* where Spinoza writes scathingly of philosophers who:

> . . . conceive of men, not as they are, but as they themselves would like them to be. Whence it has come to pass that, instead of ethics, they have generally written satire, and that they have never conceived of a theory of politics which could be turned to use, but such as might be taken for a chimera, or might have been formed in Utopia, or in that golden age of the poets when, to be sure, there was least need of it.[2]

It remains to be seen how far Rousseau will succeed in writing a political treatise that Spinoza would have deemed non-satirical. Here, at any rate, Rousseau is telling us that he is not concerned just to sketch a purely abstract picture of what an ideal state would look like, rather, he is building in a requirement of practicability from the start. A just social order that went against – or rather too flatly against – people's perceived interests would be seen by them as alien and oppressive. A legitimate social order must be one that people are capable of both living in and living with – it must not be excessively demanding.

Rousseau's insistence on taking 'men as they are' may seem puzzling to anyone already aware of his other writings, especially the *Discourse on Inequality*, since there he emphasises the way in which human character can be reshaped by education and social institutions. Must Rousseau's work then be practicable given the patterns of motivation and psychology that Rousseau finds around him in eighteenth-century Europe? A charitable approach would suggest that a theory of political justice is not required to take existing motivations as an unchangeable given, but insofar as motivations are regarded as changeable, that transformation must not be too far-fetched. As we shall see, Rousseau envisages extensive management of the passions that have emerged in humans over the course of their history, but not the outright replacement of those passions.

What are Rousseau's credentials for writing on political subjects (1.0.2)? In Book X of the *Republic* – a text which Rousseau knew very well – Plato questions Homer's knowledge of statecraft and generalship and imagines the question being put to the poet: 'Homer, ... if you're capable of knowing what ways of life make people better in private or in public, then tell us which cities are better governed because of you, as Sparta is because of Lycurgus?'[3] The same question might reasonably be put to Rousseau (and to Plato himself, notwithstanding his advising of the tyrant of Syracuse). Rousseau, who was later to draw up proposals for both Corsica and Poland himself, refers us to his Genevan citizenship. Were he a king or a legislator he would shut up and get on with ruling, but the citizen of a free city has an obligation to instruct himself. Rousseau either sycophantically or sarcastically adds that the more he studies politics, the more reason he has to love the institutions of his home city.

MAN IS BORN FREE (1.1.1–2)

'Man is born free, and everywhere he is in chains'. The *Social Contract* opens with a rhetorical flourish that is typical of Rousseauian beginnings. Seldom has a phrase been so misunderstood. To a modern reader, the phrase inevitably calls to mind another great chain-invoking line, 'Workers of the world unite! You have nothing to lose but your chains!', from the *Communist Manifesto*. In what sense were, or are, men born free? One answer is to look backwards to Rousseau's account of our natural condition of independence in the *Discourse on Inequality*. The solitary wood-wanderer of that work is certainly not bound by any laws or social ties. But we might also look to Rousseau's fellow 'social contract' theorists, Hobbes and Locke, for elucidation. All three writers want to say that our natural condition is one of non-subordination. We are born free and equal in the sense that no person has by nature the right to command any other person nor the duty to submit to the commands of another. There is no natural hierarchy in the human species, no alpha-male whom the rest of us just have to put up with as the one in charge. Human beings are normally endowed with enough reason to make them adequate as masters of themselves and need not, and should not, submit to the authority of another.

In what sense, then, are we everywhere in chains? In two, which Rousseau here runs together. The first chains that bind us are chains of law. Hobbes had used the metaphor of laws as artificial chains in *Leviathan*, telling us that men have:

> made Artificiall Chains called Civill Lawes, which they themselves, by mutuall covenants, have fastned at one end, to the lips of that Man, or Assembly, to whom they have given the Soveraigne Power; and at the other end to their own Ears.
>
> (*Leviathan*, ch. 21, p. 147)

In due course we shall see that Rousseau does not actually regard all the chains of *law* as inimical to our freedom. But true to his refusal to accept the surface appearance of freedom and equality of the fraudulent social contract of the *Discourse on Inequality*, Rousseau also has in mind chains of dependence. These come in two causally intertwined forms: material dependence, where people depend on one another for their sustenance; and psychological dependence, where people depend on the opinion of others for the satisfaction of their *amour propre*. As Rousseau continues his opening paragraph we see that his primary and negative focus is on these chains of dependence. They are both comprehensive and deceptive. He tells us that anyone who thinks themselves the master of another is more of a slave than they. This is a thought he expresses at greater length elsewhere. So, for example, in *Emile* he tells us:

> Even domination is servile when it is connected with opinion, for you depend on the prejudices of those whom you govern by prejudices . . . To lead them as you please, you must conduct yourself as they please. They have only to change their way of thinking, and you must perforce change your way of acting.[4]

As we saw in Chapter 2, this dependence on the opinion of others, epitomised by such figures as the unhappy European Minister from the *Discourse on Inequality*, is, for Rousseau, a pervasive feature of modern life.

Having told us that he does not know how the change from natural freedom and equality to servility and domination came about, Rousseau is now prepared to say, somewhat abruptly and shockingly, that he can resolve the question of how it can be made legitimate! The reader whose focus hitherto has been on relations of dependence, domination and servility is likely to wonder what is going on. Rousseau seems to be shifting back from a concern with chains of dependence to the chains of law. Our natural freedom in the form of complete independence is lost (and lost forever). Rousseau will argue that there is, nevertheless, a form of subordination – subordination to law – that can sometimes be morally justified and, indeed, that he can provide the required justification for it.

The immediately following paragraph provides us with an outline of Rousseau's project in Book 1 of *Du Contrat Social*. His purpose in that book is to reject two possible sources of social order: force and nature. He believes that, once he has done this, 'convention' or agreement is the only remaining candidate as a possible source of legitimacy. The project of rejecting nature as the source of social order is to be accomplished in Chapter 2, and that of rejecting force in Chapter 3. In Chapters 4, 5 and 6, Rousseau will go on to outline the nature of the conventions that initiate and constitute the new political order.

THE GENERAL SOCIETY OF THE HUMAN RACE
(*Geneva Manuscript* ch. 2)

We must now take a brief detour from the published text of the *Social Contract*. The famous 'Man was born free' beginning gives a striking impact to the start of the book, but in Rousseau's earlier draft – the *Geneva Manuscript* – those words appear at the beginning of Chapter 3. In that text they were preceded by an important discussion that Rousseau excised from the final version but which nevertheless provides us with a conceptual bridge between the world of the *Discourse on Inequality* and the *Social Contract*. That chapter, entitled 'Of the General Society of the Human Race' is both a brief sketch of human historical development and a critique of an article by Rousseau's one-time friend Denis Diderot. We need to look first at Diderot's piece to get the context for Rousseau's own response.

In 1755, Denis Diderot had published an article in the *Encyclopédie* on the topic of 'Natural Right'. This appeared, in fact, in the very same volume that contained Rousseau's entry on 'Political Economy'. Diderot's text is not particularly original, being a warmed-over version of ideas from Pufendorf and others. The details should not detain us too long. The central interest lies in Diderot's attempt to respond to a kind of moral sceptic who sees what the demands of justice are but sees no reason to comply with them. This figure is clearly a descendant of characters like Thrasymachus from Plato's *Republic* and the Foole from Hobbes's *Leviathan*. Diderot's 'violent interlocutor' renounces mutually advantageous rules of conduct, to become a moral outlaw willing to take his chances with a regime that would permit predatory conduct on their part at the risk of being preyed upon by others. Would such a person be reasonable or unreasonable? Diderot argues that the interlocutor's suggestion fails to meet a test of reciprocity. There is no reason to believe that others will find the rule such a person proposes acceptable: the individual who puts forward such a principle has a strictly limited exposure to costs (since he only has one life) and yet claims a permission to make himself master of an unlimited number of others. He is also, claims Diderot, judge in his own cause. Diderot has yet to say anything about the content of the rules of justice that the 'violent interlocutor' might refuse to be bound by.

In a rather breathtaking leap of reasoning, Diderot asks where a tribunal competent to determine the nature of justice can be found and answers that humanity as a whole is such a tribunal. The human race as such has no desire other than for the common good. Whereas individual wills may be 'suspect', the general will of humanity as a whole 'is always good'. In a striking anticipation of modern contractarian theories, he suggests that this tribunal might take the form of a hypothetical assembly, to which other creatures and species might be summoned if, like us, they were possessed of the faculty of reason. For Diderot the 'general will' of such a hypothetical assembly establishes rules of justice which amount to the position that each person is to enjoy those rights that are compatible with a like enjoyment of rights by others. Happily, we do not have to engage in the thought-experiment of the hypothetical assembly, or, if we do, we can check its results against a body of existing practice. We can consult the general will of the human race:

> In the principles of prescribed law of all civilised nations; in the social practices of savage and barbarous peoples; in the tacit agreements obtaining amongst the enemies of mankind; and even in those two emotions – indignation and resentment – which nature has extended as far as animals to compensate for social laws and public retribution.[5]

Diderot concludes his article with nine theses. The most important of these for our purposes is that 'the general will is in each person a pure expression of the understanding, which in the silence of the passions calculates what every individual may demand of his fellow-man, and what his fellow-man has a right to demand of him'. This general will should regulate the conduct of individuals towards one another, towards the societies to which they belong and of those societies towards other societies.

Rousseau's reaction to this discussion in Chapter 2 of the *Geneva Manuscript* has a tone of incredulity. At the centre of his argument is a distinction which Diderot has failed to make between the content of justice and the motive to be just. Rousseau has an 'independent man' – the same character as Diderot's 'violent interlocutor' – react to Diderot's suggestion that he can consult the general will of the human race as a guide to conduct:

> 'I admit that I do, indeed, see that this is the rule which I can consult; but I still do not see,' our independent man will say, 'the reason for subjecting myself to this rule. It is not a matter of teaching me what justice is; it is a matter of showing me what interest I have in being just.'
>
> (G2: 157/OC3: 286)

Rousseau continues, reproducing some of Diderot's own words:

> . . . no one will deny that the general will is in each individual a pure act of the understanding reasoning in the silence of the passions about what man may demand of his fellow man, and about what his fellow man may rightfully demand of him: But where is the man who can thus separate himself from himself and, if care for one's self-preservation is the first precept of nature, can he be forced thus to consider the species in general in order to impose on himself duties whose connection with his own constitution he completely fails to see?
>
> (G2: 157/OC3: 286)

Rousseau's thought here is that the abstractions of universal and mutually beneficial rules of conduct are insufficient to motivate the conduct of individuals in circumstances that resemble a Hobbesian state of nature, a state that Rousseau believes will more or less have arisen as a consequence of historical development. Rousseau is thus denying what Diderot is implicitly affirming, namely, that a judgement of what justice requires is sufficient to motivate an agent to action. What is unclear on first reading is whether this is just a psychological claim, or whether Rousseau believes that the 'independent man' is correct in refusing to recognise reasons of justice as sufficient reasons for action, or in error. We shall return to that question in a moment. But first let us have a look at the development of Rousseau's own argument.

Rousseau begins with a brief account of how and why he believes the need for political institutions has arisen. The most primitive humans, presumably the wood-wandering solitary individuals of the *Discourse on Inequality*, have, as individuals, natural abilities and needs that are perfectly balanced. Consequently, they have no need of one another. As human needs expand, though, people need one another's help and co-operation to attain what they want. Rousseau's text here suggests something like a prisoner's dilemma or similar collective action problem. All desire the fruits of social co-operation but each person will, if he can, seek to enjoy those fruits at the expense of others while contributing little or nothing himself. Life quickly becomes a struggle for competitive advantage and though the patterns of co-operation we establish create, for the first time, a 'general society', it is a society that is, consequently, in flux and which offers no peace or security to the individual.

Although this 'general society' is a nightmare for the individuals within it, the option of returning to the truly primitive state is unavailable to them. Even if it were available, Rousseau tells us that it would be defective from the moral point of view. The disconnectedness of primitive humans prevented their cognitive development: the interconnected society, though it brings forth human vice, also makes virtue possible. At least *potentially*, humans can taste 'the most delicious sentiment of the soul, which is the love of virtue'. Rousseau's discussion now becomes somewhat confusing since he uses the phrase 'state of independence' to denote a stage of human development which is later than the state of 'perfect independence' that he had earlier referred to. The later 'state of independence' is a state in which people have no authority over one another but where they do have social interaction. For Rousseau, this stage is broadly Hobbesian in character. Indeed, his discussion resembles Hobbes's own discussion of the 'laws of nature'. As Hobbes puts it:

... he that should be modest, and tractable, and performe all he promises, in such time, and place, where no man els should do so, should but make himselfe a prey to others, and procure his own certain ruine, contrary to the ground of all Lawes of Nature, which tend to Natures preservation.

(*Leviathan*, ch. 25, p. 110)

The 'independent man' whom Rousseau now borrows from Diderot prefers to rely on his own strength, to take his chances, rather than to subordinate himself to a universal morality. Whereas Diderot seeks traces of the general will in the conduct of nations, Rousseau offers the aggressive and acquisitive behaviour of states towards one another as evidence that the 'independent man' would have reasoned as he suggests.

Like Diderot, Rousseau asks us what answer can be given to the reasoning of such a person. It is, he suggests, useless to appeal to religion. Most people have been immune to the influence of 'the sublime notions of the God of the wise' and insofar as they have been susceptible to religious influence this has been as much at the service of selfishness, and indeed murder, as of peace and good order. Nor, as we have seen, does Rousseau find Diderot's philosopher's answer adequate, precisely because it fails to engage with the independent man's own perception of his self-interest. Diderot's answer is doubly implausible because it requires human beings to form an idea of the general will of the human race based, perhaps, on the notion of a hypothetical assembly of humanity in order that they may associate peacefully together. But, far from the particular associations in which human beings participate being an application in the specific case of general moral principles, Rousseau argues that the ideas of universal morality can only arise as a generalisation from particular experiences and histories.[6]

What, then, is to be done? Rousseau concedes that there is *nothing* that can be *said* by way of argument to convince the independent man. Rather, what is needed is action rather than argument: the construction of new institutions that will both show by example their superiority to the neo-Hobbesian order and which will transform individuals so that they can correctly identify their own interest. Rousseau declares: 'Let us show him in perfected art the redress of the evils which beginning art caused to nature'(G2: 159/OC3: 287). He is suggesting that while the growth of artificial passions and rational calculation has destroyed the primitive harmony enjoyed by the 'stupid and limited animal' of the first ages, the correction of the ills thus caused is to be the task of well-directed artifice and right reason. The task of the rest of the *Social Contract* will be to set out the nature of the artifice that is necessary to achieve man's possibilities as an intelligent being by putting 'goodness in our hearts' and 'morality in our actions' and enabling us to achieve the love of virtue.

Some critics have suggested that Rousseau deleted this chapter from the final version of the *Social Contract* because the Hobbesian character of his response to Diderot makes the transition to a just society extremely implausible.[7] Others have argued that the chapter marks a rejection of universal moral standards on Rousseau's part in favour of purely local ones: the general wills of particular societies.[8] The first of these concerns brings to the surface a genuine difficulty, and one of which Rousseau was himself aware. The perfected state which is to serve as an example to the 'violent inter-locutor' will first have to be built in order to fulfil its function: but who is going to build it? This is an issue that Rousseau confronts later in the *Social Contract* in his discussion of the lawgiver (2.7), which we shall come to presently. It is, though, a serious misreading of Rousseau's argument to see him as endorsing either a Hobbesian reading or some form of moral relativism. The final paragraph of the chapter suggests that Rousseau believes the independent man to be making a *mistake*, but a mistake that cannot be corrected by *argument* but only by the force of example: 'Let us show him . . . all that is *false* in the reasoning which he believed solid' (G2: 159/OC3: 228, emphasis added).

In fact, Diderot and Rousseau both believe in the existence of universal standards of right. But for Rousseau, the appeal to such standards in a condition of fear and insecurity is a vain one. Later in the *Geneva Manuscript*, Rousseau explains how membership in a civil association, by giving each individual a sense of personal security makes it possible for people to start treating non-members of their own society according to standards of justice similar to those that have evolved within it. The laws within particular societies promote the common good of the citizens who are moved to develop dispositions to civility, beneficence and virtue.

> Extend this maxim to the general society of which the State gives us the idea, protected by the society of which we are members, or by that in which we live, the natural revulsion to do evil no longer being offset by the fear of having evil done to us, we are inclined at once, by nature, by habit by reason, to deal at once with other men more or less as [we do] with our fellow-citizens, and this disposition reduced to actions gives rise to the rules of reasoned natural right, different from natural right properly so called, which is founded on nothing but a true but very vague sentiment often stifled by the love of ourselves.
>
> (G2: 160/OC3: 329)

As Grace G. Roosevelt puts it. 'After we gain a context of trust, . . . it is possible that our concept of justice will extend to include others who do not happen to belong to our own community.'[9] Membership in a particular society is not, then, a licence for chauvinism, it gives us the possibility, for the first time, of acting according to the dictates of reason and conscience by freeing us from the grip of competition and insecurity. But the path to this possibility of becoming moral and rational creatures does not lie through moral argument: it lies through the construction of new social and political environments through which we can become citizens.

NOTES

1 Interestingly, this statement of intent differs appreciably from the parallel passage in the *Geneva Manuscript*, where Rousseau tells us that 'There is no question here of the administration of this body, but rather of its constitution'. But this difference is not of any great significance once we appreciate that Rousseau is not, here, talking of a rule to be applied *in* administration, but rather of rules to which any administration must be subordinate.

2   Spinoza, *A Political Treatise*, p. 287.

3   Republic X, 599d, Plato, *Complete Works*. Rousseau's precis/translation of *Republic* X, 'De l'imitation théatrale' was written in preparation for the *Letter to D'Alembert* and is included at OC5:1195–1211.

4   See E2: 83/OC4: 308 (cf. also the eighth *Letter from the Mountain* at OC3: 841). My thinking in this paragraph is very much influenced by Strong, *Jean-Jacques Rousseau*, pp. 68–9.

5   Diderot, *Political Writings*, p. 20.

6   It is less than clear from Rousseau's discussion here what he takes himself to have established. Is he making a claim about how we come to have knowledge of general moral principles – that is a psychological or epistemic thesis – or is he trying to say something about the logical relationship between general principles and their applications? It may well be that in order to come to know general principles we have to generalise from particular applications. But that hardly suffices to establish that the general principles are not logically prior to the particular ones.

7   See, for example, Riley, *The General Will Before Rousseau*, pp. 202–3.

8   See Gourevitch, 'Recent Work on Rousseau', pp. 536–56.

9   Roosevelt, *Reading Rousseau in the Nuclear Age*, p. 88. Roosevelt devotes a chapter-length discussion to Rousseau's dispute with Diderot and I have learnt much from it.

4

FALSE THEORIES OF
THE BODY POLITIC

(Book 1, Chs 3–5)

Before Rousseau can set out his own views on political legitimacy
and authority, he has to deal with what were regarded in his
own time as competing theories to the view that political authority
is derived from the consent of the governed. Rousseau's argument
here is partly an argument by elimination. He believes that if he
succeeds in demolishing theories that either accord some the right
to rule by nature or assert the right of the stronger, then something like his own view will be vindicated by default: 'Since no man
has a natural authority over his fellow-man, and since force produces
no right, conventions remain as the basis of all legitimate authority
among men' (1.4.1) (see also 1.1.2).

As a general mode of argument, this is not very convincing. If I
want to justify some proposition, P, and can think of four possible
arguments for P (A, B, C and D), it will hardly be sufficient to
justify D that A, B and C all fail. In the first place, it may just be
that there is *no justification at all* for P so that all arguments in its
favour will fail. Second, it may be that I have failed – through lack
of imagination – to exhaust the list of possible arguments in favour

of P, so that there is some further argument, E, that I have not considered. But whatever the merits of Rousseau's approach here, we need to consider the particular views he discusses.

First, though, we need to be clear about what these theories purport to be theories of. They are theories of legitimate state authority, meaning that they are theories that purport to justify the proposition that states have the right to issue binding commands to their subjects, commands that subjects have a duty to obey.[1] When subjects accept that states have authority over them, they accept by that fact that properly issued commands of states in the form of laws or other directives ought rightly to pre-empt their own deliberations about what they have most reason to do. They must do as the state says, quite independently of their own views on the subject at hand.

Rousseau considers three broad families of justification for political authority in Book 1. First, he looks at theories of natural subordination, both patriarchal and natural-aristocratic. Second, he looks at the so-called 'right of the stronger'. Third, he looks at the possibility that authority might be justified by some agreement. He considers two types of agreement. First, a pact of submission, whereby subordinates would accept the authority of a master and second, an agreement among equals. Having rejected natural aristocracy, the right of the stronger and a pact of submission, Rousseau believes that he has made space for his own preferred view.

NATURAL SUBORDINATION (1.2)

In Chapter 2 of Book 1, Rousseau attacks two views that trace legitimate authority back to *nature*. When he does this, it is important to bear in mind that he is not referring us back to the *state of nature* such as he discusses in the *Discourse on Inequality*. Rather, he is inquiring whether there is anything in the nature of human beings that can justify some people being subject to the authority of others. His first target here is theories that treat the legitimacy of the state as being like the authority of a father within a family. Second, he looks at theories that base it on natural differences among human beings: his principal target in the latter case is Aristotle's theory of natural slavery.

The theory that state authority derives from paternal authority might take two forms. Either these theories suppose that state authority just *is* paternal authority, alternatively they may be suggesting that it is *like* paternal authority in some way. This justification for the legitimate authority of the state is most famously found in the *Patriarcha* of Sir Robert Filmer. Filmer's arguments were attacked by Locke in the second of his *Two Treatises of Government*, and Rousseau does little here to add to Locke's arguments except to emphasise the more Hobbesian aspects of Locke's view. In the first paragraph of Chapter 2, Rousseau declares that the family is 'the most ancient and the only natural' form of society. Here, he is simply repeating Locke's claim that the authority of fathers over their children is derived from the need of the children and ceases when that need ceases:

> *Children*, I confess are not borne in this full state of *Equality*, though they are born to it. Their Parents have a sort of Rule and Jurisdiction over them when they come into the World, and for some time after, but tis but a temporary one. The Bonds of this Subjection are like the Swaddling Cloths they are wrapt up in, and supported by, in the weakness of their Infancy. Age and Reason, as they grow up, loosen them till at length they drop quite off, and leave a Man at his own free Disposal.
>
> (Locke, *Second Treatise*: §55, in Locke,
> *Two Treatises of Government*)

Children, then, incapable of being responsible exercisers of choice, are naturally subject to the authority of their parents. But this is a temporary condition. When they become capable of making decisions for themselves they acquire the right to decide for themselves. Sometimes, as both Locke and Rousseau testify, children continue to accord authority to their father beyond their childhood. This, however, is a matter of agreement. The origin of this authority is a voluntary concession of right to the father on the part of the children. This voluntary submission to paternal authority may, if it rests on a tacit rather than an explicit agreement, give rise to the impression that authority has a natural basis. But force of habit, tradition and the natural saliency of the father as a source of authority are generating a false impression of what is really going on.

Rousseau's reproduction of Locke's argument in the first three paragraphs of Book 1, Chapter 2, suggests, at least by implication, that he endorses the idea that the morally primitive condition of people is one where they enjoy a natural (meaning here just non- or pre-conventional) right to liberty. This follows from the fact that he allows that paternal authority may be established by voluntary or conventional means. Only persons who were already in possession of a right to determine their own actions and to be free from the interference of others could cede or waive such rights in favour of others.

Where Rousseau's emphasis differs a little from Locke's is when he tells us at 1.2.2 that the independence that all men gain on reaching the age of reason is justified by the 'first law' which is to 'provide for his own preservation'. This has seemed to some to be a rather Hobbesian importation into the theory,[2] and might be thought to raise difficulties as soon as Rousseau tells us the liberty he gains is based in the fact that each adult person is a sufficiently competent judge of the means of their preservation and that this is why they become their own master on attaining the age of reason (1.2.2). For this is surely an empirical matter. Why should it be automatically the case that individuals better achieve the end of self-preservation by relying on their own judgement than by submitting themselves to the authority of another – such as a Hobbesian absolute sovereign?

Rousseau says little here to reassure us on this point. But he does indicate a basic disanalogy between paternal and political authority: motivation. A father exercising paternal power has only to consult his natural affections for his children, whereas this cannot be assumed in the case of the chief. In the *Geneva Manuscript*, Rousseau expands further on this difference, telling us:

> . . . if the voice of nature is the best counsel that a father must listen to if he is to fulfil his duties, it is for the Magistrate nothing but a false guide which works ceaselessly to divert him from his, and which

drags him, sooner or later to his downfall or to that of the State, unless he is held back by prudence or virtue. . . . To do well, the first only has to consult his heart; the other becomes a traitor the moment he listen to his.

(OC3: 300)

The natural affection of fathers for their children is not, then, just inoperative in the political case, it is actually a *vice* since those in political authority are required to be impartial towards their subjects. Paternal affection leads to nepotism rather than justice. Since such a ruler will often not have the best interest of his subjects at heart, accepting his authority may not, in fact, be a good means of preserving oneself and obeying that first law of nature.

Rousseau's discussion hitherto has presupposed that the best interests of the governed must figure somehow in the justification of political authority. He now goes on to mention in a somewhat cursory and derisive manner, two theories that allegedly reject that assumption: those of Hobbes and Grotius. (He returns to a more considered rejection of their views at 1.4.) These two thinkers were important points of reference for Rousseau at various stages of his career, but while he appears to have made a positive revaluation of Hobbes as a philosopher by 1762, his estimation of Grotius had plummeted by then. Grotius's *De Juri Belli ac Pacis* is one of the founding treatises of modern international law and, through his translator Barbeyrac, Grotius exercised a significant influence on Enlightenment thinking. Rousseau mentions him thirteen times in the *Social Contract*, far more than any other modern thinker. In the 'Epistle Dedicatory' of the *Discourse on Inequality*, Rousseau recalls his father: 'I see him still, living off the work of his hands and nourishing his soul with the most sublime Truths. I see Tacitus, Plutarch and Grotius before him amidst the tools of his trade' (G1: 120/OC3: 118).

But by the time Rousseau had come to draft the *Social Contract*, his view of Grotius had changed profoundly. He had come to see Grotius as little more than an apologist for the excesses of kings and princes. In *Emile* he makes the following comment:

The science of political right is yet to be born, and it is to be presumed that it never will be born. Grotius, the master of all our learned men in this matter, is only a child and, what is worse, a child of bad faith. When I hear Grotius praised to the skies and Hobbes covered with execration, I see how few sensible men read or understand these two authors. The truth is that their two principles are exactly alike.

(E5: 458/OC4: 836)

In the *Social Contract* Rousseau presents both Hobbes and Grotius as believing that the human race is to be considered as so many herds of cattle being fattened for the benefit of a ruler. But this was certainly unfair to Hobbes. Rather, Hobbes believed that the goal of self-preservation – which, after all, Rousseau has just endorsed (1.1.2) – is best served by submission to an absolute ruler.

Grotius is another matter. The fact is that it is difficult to derive any consistent position from the rag-bag that is *De Juri Belli ac Pacis*. Rousseau's claim that Grotius's 'most frequent method of argument is always to establish right by fact' cannot be dismissed as unfair in the way that his remarks on Hobbes can. In seeking to answer whether some practice is permissible by natural law, Grotius's procedure often seems to amount to little more than a trawl through history and through ancient authorities and scripture to find some evidence of the practice going on – if he can find it that seems to satisfy him that it is indeed permissible.[3] So, for example, in Book 3 Chapter 4 of his work he discussed the permissibility of slaughtering the women and children of a defeated party. Granting that we may not draw wider inferences from cases where God himself has directly made His will manifest, Grotius nevertheless argues that there are many other recorded instances, in Hebrew, Greek and Roman history where such massacre took place: 'Titus sentenced the women and children of the Jews to be torn by wild beasts in the arena.'[4] To be sure, such practices are to be condemned as barbarous, but the issue here for Grotius is their permissibility under the law of nations, and for this such precedents seem to suffice. In attacking Hobbes and Grotius, Rousseau even goes so far as to compare them to a figure of universal ill-repute, the Emperor Caligula. Caligula had reasoned that 'kings were gods, or that peoples were beasts' (1.2.6).

But there is a view that Rousseau feels he has to treat with a little more respect, namely that promoted by Aristotle, suggesting that some are born for slavery and others to rule. Aristotle had argued, at the very beginning of the *Politics* that:

> ... there must necessarily be a union of the naturally ruling element with the element which is naturally ruled, for the preservation of both. The element which is able, by virtue of its intelligence, to exercise forethought is naturally a ruling and master element; the element which is able, by virtue of its bodily power, to do what the other element plans is a ruled element, which is naturally in a state of slavery; and master and slave have accordingly a common interest.[5]

Rousseau responds to Aristotle, not by arguing directly for fundamental human equality but, rather, by giving a qualified agreement to Aristotle's account of the fact that has the effect of undermining his argument for natural aristocracy. Aristotle, he tells us was right. But this is a consequence of the plasticity of human nature. If there are unjust social institutions, then there will be human types that are adapted to that injustice and inequality.

> Slaves lose everything in their chains, even the desire of escaping from them: they love their servitude, as the comrades of Ulysses loved their brutish conditions. If then there are slaves by nature, it is because there have been slaves against nature. Force made the first slaves, and their cowardice perpetuated the condition.
>
> (1.2.8)

It is hard to know whether or not Rousseau is right about the attitude of most slaves. Certainly it would be unwise to take their public declarations of affection for their masters as evidence of their real attitudes. Slaves who say such things may simply be making a rational response to the balance of forces facing them.[6] On the other hand, there is evidence that many slaves adapt psychologically to the relationship of forces by some kind of acceptance of the legitimacy of their subordination.[7] Rousseau's response underlines that we cannot take acceptance of the authority of some by the many as evidence for the moral legitimacy of the few. It also reminds us of one of the great themes of the *Social Contract*, a theme taken up by later thinkers such as Hegel and Marx, namely that the kind of people there are, and the attitudes and behaviour they exhibit, is profoundly affected by the nature of the social and authority relations they find themselves subject to.

Rousseau does not, though, argue *directly* against theories of natural aristocracy. As we shall see later he is prepared to accept, and indeed to rely upon, extraordinary variations in ability within the human species. But such are remarkable flashes of ability in untypical individuals rather than predictable and enduring divisions among humans. Many people have subscribed to a view like Aristotle's in which there is supposed to be a natural hierarchy among human beings such that some have natural authority over others for common benefit. Such a view is, however, deeply implausible on empirical grounds. In the first place, it is unlikely that the ability to plan and to exercise forethought is reducible to a single dimension of intelligence such that we could easily sort out those suited to command from those suited to obey. Notoriously, for example, many academics are persons of great intelligence who nevertheless have poor organisational and social skills. Second, there is the question of the identification of leaders. Clearly there are going to be various racist and sexist theories purporting to sort people in the categories of naturally dominant and naturally subordinate, but there is no empirical basis to support such views. In the absence of a natural mark of dominance, how are we going to decide who rules? And who is to decide? Self-selection is clearly a bad idea, since the class of those who believe themselves suited by nature to rule is going to be much larger than the class of those actually best equipped to rule. The boorish self-promoting person will probably have a great advantage over the intelligent but diffident one. Given that the interest of all are at stake and that we have no a priori way of identifying the best, it seems that any principle of natural hierarchy is either going to be unworkable or is going to express itself through the everyday working of institutions that are open to all so long as there is fair equality of opportunity.

Elsewhere in Rousseau's work, we do sometimes find an endorsement of natural inequalities that is anything but contingent and episodic. In a remarkable lapse from the attitude expressed in his remarks about Aristotle, Rousseau himself endorses a 'natural aristocracy' approach when he comes to discuss relations between the sexes, arguing that 'woman is made to please and to be subjugated'.[8] This is not the place to discuss Rousseau's views on men and women in detail, but we should note that his observation that servile natures are often the consequence rather than the cause and justification of domination can be just as well applied to his own sexist views.

Rousseau ends his chapter on natural subordination by a further ironic swipe at Filmer and his ilk on the theory of patriarchal authority. Here, his target is not theories that attempt to ground political authority on an *analogy* with paternal power but, rather, the claim that political authority just *is* paternal power. It might be, Rousseau jokingly suggests, that if an accurate genealogy of the human race were constructed, Rousseau might find himself installed as king through direct descent from Adam. He thereby highlights the substantial epistemic problems faced by the theory of patriarchal power. In fact, he says, the domination of one person over another needs justification and cannot be established from natural facts. Robinson Crusoe was king over his island, but as soon as he discovered a footprint in the sand it was necessary to establish any title to rule on a new basis.

THE RIGHT OF THE STRONGER (1.3)

Having rejected theories that find some natural basis for legitimate subordination of some by others, another option has to be to reason from the fact of political power to the right to command. Rousseau believes that this is an unrealistic strategy and an insufficient basis for a stable political order. As he points out: 'The stronger is never strong enough to be forever master, unless he transforms his force into right, and obedience into duty' (1.3.1).

The stronger (as Hobbes would readily have acknowledged) can never dominate the weaker simply by force alone: subordinates have to be convinced that they *ought* to obey. Rousseau, here, gives a basic motivation for theories of *ideology* and authority, laying the groundwork for Hegel, Marx, Nietzsche and Weber. Force is always insufficient, only the voluntary acceptance of rule by the subordinated can provide an adequate guarantee of stability.

Further, if you can dominate people by force then there is no need to claim the right to do so. If right flows from force, then as soon as the balance of force changes, then so does the balance of right. Both in saying this, and in lampooning St Paul (Romans 13: 1), Rousseau echoes Montesquieu's *Persian Letters*, where the protagonist Usbek writes of the English:

> The crime of high treason, according to them, is simply a crime committed by a weaker party against a stronger by disobeying, whatever form this disobedience takes. Thus the English people, finding themselves the stronger party in a conflict with one of their kings, declared that it was a crime of high treason for a prince to make war on his subjects. They have therefore good reasons for saying that the precept in their Koran, to be subject to the powers that be, is not very difficult to follow, since it is impossible for them not to follow it; and the more so because they are not required to submit to whoever is the most virtuous, but to the strongest.[9]

While it is difficult for modern readers to take the doctrine of passive obedience seriously, we should be aware that such an attitude was widely promoted in Rousseau's own day and earlier. We can find it in Bossuet and indeed in Pascal. Rousseau makes some more derisive comments about such apologists for power at the end of 3.6 (on monarchy).

Is Rousseau too dismissive about the argument from de facto power? A Hobbesian counter-argument might run as follows: stable government is a very great good and ensures that we are not in a state of war where no-one can prosper and life is 'nasty, brutish and short'. Rousseau himself has suggested that the state of nature *ends up* being like this, in both the *Discourse on Inequality* and in

'The General Society of the Human Race'. The 'independent man' of the latter, knows what the 'general will' – in this context akin to Hobbes's laws of nature – requires. But, under the circumstance of a universal state of war, prudence dictates non-compliance with those laws. An authority – pretty much any authority – might change this situation by providing everyone with a guarantee of peaceful conduct and the keeping of agreements. If this is right, then the 'right of the stronger', by making some authority *salient* would provide each person with a prudential reason for recognising de facto power in a way that would strengthen and entrench that very power. To be sure, Rousseau can correctly point out that the right extends no longer than the power does. But the basis for that right over each individual is not just effective power over that individual, but a guarantee to each individual of effective power over each other individual. This is, of course, much much less than the putative advocate of the 'right of the stronger' wants, since it does not ground a right to rule. Nevertheless, it does provide a rational basis for the acceptance of such rule, not simply because the individual's best course of action faced with effective power is to obey, but also because the common knowledge of such obedience provides each person with assurance about the behaviour of each other person.

Why would Rousseau reject such a system? Essentially, because security is not what he values most. Although such de facto state power would, at least in the best of cases, assure the security and even the material prosperity of all subjects, Rousseau believes that it would leave each person vulnerable to the capricious will of another particular human being. Since he believes that our most fundamental interest is an interest in *freedom*, he will reject this solution. This becomes clear in the immediately following section.

OF SLAVERY (1.4)

If there is no legitimate authority by nature and none from force alone, what then remains? According to Rousseau, there is just one candidate: convention. But perhaps the form an agreement could take would be one where a subordinate voluntarily subjects himself to a master? Rousseau's discussion here is in two parts. First (1.4.2–6) he discusses a properly voluntary pact of submission and concludes that it is contrary to the core human interest in freedom and that the agreement by which such submission would be made is conceptually flawed. Second (1.4.7–12) he attacks the idea put forward by both Grotius and Hobbes that victory in war can be the basis for a just (and contractual) subordination of the defeated.

Grotius, Rousseau tells us, discussed the possibility that just as an individual may alienate his freedom and become a slave voluntarily, then perhaps a whole people could. The relevant passage is part of Grotius's rejection of 'the opinion of those who maintain that everywhere and without exception, the sovereignty lies in the people':

> By both the Jewish and Roman Law, any man may legitimately submit himself in private slavery to whomever he pleases. Why then may not an independent people submit itself to one or more persons, completely transferring to them its right to govern itself?[10]

But according to Rousseau, this suggestion is just an absurdity. He offers us an analysis of the word 'alienate', meaning to give or to sell and asks what the motive of a people could possible be to give or sell themselves.[11] An individual, at the limit, he suggests might be pressed by the need to subsist, perhaps to escape a famine, to enter into such an agreement. But why would a people do so? After all, says Rousseau, it is kings who derive their subsistence from their subjects and not vice versa.

Alternatively, he suggests, in reference to Hobbes, that the motive might be 'civil tranquility'. Here (1.4.3) he ends up, once again, paraphrasing a passage from Locke's *Second Treatise*:

> Who would not think it an admirable Peace betwixt the Mighty and the Mean, when the Lamb, without resistance, yielded his Throat to be torn by the imperious Wolf? *Polyphemus's* Den gives us a perfect Pattern of such a Peace, and such a Government, wherein *Ulysses* and his companions had nothing to do, but quietly to suffer themselves to be devour'd. And no doubt *Ulysses*, who was a prudent Man,

preach'd up *Passive Obedience*, and exhorted them to a quiet Submission, by representing to them of what concernment Peace was to Mankind; and by shewing the inconveniencies might happen, if they should offer to resist *Polyphemus*, who had now the power over them.
(Locke, *Second Treatise*: §228)[12]

In addition, Rousseau has four supplementary arguments against the idea that political authority could be based upon a contract between governors and subordinates. First, he argues that, since such a contract is contrary to any conceiveable interest that a person has, to enter into it is to give evidence of madness and a contract entered into in a state of madness is invalid. Second, he argues that since parents could not bind their children by such an agreement, any such contract would need to be renewed in each generation. But this would be to dissolve the basis for government which was both arbitrary and legitimate, since its arbitrary character would disappear. That is to say that if renewal in each generation is needed, the partisans of absolutist power get something other than what they want since sovereignty will, in fact, continue to reside with the people. Third, he argues that a contract involving the renunciation of liberty is incompatible with the nature of man. He says that to deprive oneself of free choice is to abandon the responsibility for one's actions that gives them a moral character. Finally, he argues that there is no sense to any agreement which stipulates absolute obedience by one party and accords unlimited authority to the other. What would count as a breach of this agreement by the superior party? Absolutely nothing.

Rousseau's first argument – that it is so plainly contrary to a person's interest to enter into an agreement that reduced them to the status of a slave that doing so is evidence of contract-invalidating insanity, is surely wrong. It appears to contradict what he has already told us at 1.4.2 about a person giving themselves for their subsistence. Someone might well submit to slavery in order to secure the welfare of some other person that they cared about. For instance, a mother might do so to ensure the survival of her children. But Rousseau is surely right to reject such contracts as possible bases of *political* authority.

His second argument is that even if such an agreement were possible, it would only bind those party to it and not succeeding generations. Here (1.4.5) he refers back to the Lockean argument of 1.2.1, that parental authority is only temporary and that children gain natural independence when they have reached the age of reason. Making such a move here may be storing up trouble for the future. Rousseau is moving towards his own convention to establish political authority (1.6) and he may be just as vulnerable to this line of argument as the thinkers he is criticising. Either that, or we may be forced to conclude that the basis of authority and obligation is something other than a contract.

Rousseau's third argument – that to renounce one's freedom is to renounce one's essential humanity – is of the very greatest importance, but he compresses it here to little more than a slogan (1.4.6). Here again, we have a clue to the nature of the legitimate social order that Rousseau will argue for: it must be compatible with human freedom.

His fourth argument – that a contract to enslave oneself is an impossibility because of its one-sided nature – paraphrases a passage from Montesquieu that refers *not* to people in a natural state before the institution of civil government but, rather, to the practice of Roman debtors selling themselves and includes the intriguing suggestion that the loss of liberty to the individual constitutes a loss to the body politic as a whole. Montesquieu writes:

> Neither is it true that a freeman can sell himself. Sale implies a price; now when a person sells himself, his whole substance immediately devolves to his master; the master, therefore, in that case, gives nothing, and the slave receives nothing. ... The freedom of every citizen constitutes a part of the public liberty. ... To sell one's freedom is so repugnant to all reason as can scarcely be supposed in any man.[13]

Rousseau's own presentation of this argument suggests that a contract to sell oneself into slavery is a conceptual impossibility since no real exchange takes place. He does not really establish this here, though, since, as we have seen, the contract might be entered into for the benefit of a third party. Rousseau had written earlier that 'a man who enslaves himself to another does not give himself, he sells himself' (1.4.2), but here he is saying that selling oneself is also an impossibility. In fact, both modes of transfer seem logically problematic, though not for the reasons Rousseau advances. As Hillel Steiner has argued:

> *abandonment* of this right [of self-ownership] is the only possible mode of incurring self-enslavement. . . . That is, it cannot be incurred by a self-owner's *transferring* (selling, donating) that right, since such transfers entail that transferors thereby acquire duties to their transferees, whereas slaves, as things wholly owned by others, must lack duties as well as rights.[14]

Rousseau's second target is an argument for voluntary submission, which he attributes directly to Grotius although it is probably most familiar from Hobbes. This argument purports to justify sovereign authority on the basis of a contract between conquerors and those they defeat, whereby the vanquished agree to accept the authority in return for their lives. This position is set out by Grotius's translator Barbeyrac, whose edition of Grotius was the one Rousseau was familiar with:

> . . . the power of a master over slaves taken in this way does not originate only in custom. If a prisoner of war found that his conditions as a slave were too harsh, it was up to him to avoid them by indicating that he did not wish to recognise as his master the person who had captured him. . . . All that this amounted to was that he was courting the consequences of exposing himself to the fury of the enemy, and of losing his life for fear of losing his freedom. But if the prisoner made no declaration of intent contrary to the accepted custom between enemy peoples, he was thereby deemed to have submitted to it tacitly.[15]

Rousseau argues, distilling material from his unpublished text, *The State of War* into a few paragraphs,[16] that one person's authority over another could not arise in this manner in the state of nature. It is true that individuals in a state of nature may come into conflict with one another intermittently. But that hardly constitutes the kind of stable relationship that makes for a state of war: one of constant preparedness and mutual expectation. War, in the appropriate sense, presupposes – according to Rousseau – the prior existence of states. In any case, he tells us, war between states always makes a sharp distinction between the public character of the contending parties and the private individuals who happen to be citizens or subjects of those states. According to Rousseau, private individuals should be respected in their persons and property as far as possible. Where states go beyond this and pretend to subject the citizens of neighbouring states to their rule by force, all we really have is an extension of the so-called right of the stronger – in which case authority only persists so long as states have effective power and slaves have the right to escape or disobey when they can.[17]

There are several problems with Rousseau's argument that war is an institutional and not an interpersonal relationship. The first worry is one of consistency. Elsewhere, notably in the *Discourse on Inequality*, he seems happy to employ the language of war when it is clear from context that he is talking about a generalised state of violent disorder among individuals. So, for example, he announces in the *Discourse* that the pre-political state eventually degenerates to a point where:

> Nascent Society gave way to the most horrible state of war: Humankind, debased and devastated, no longer able to turn back or to renounce its wretched acquisitions, and working only to its shame by the abuse of the faculties that do it honor, brought itself to the brink of ruin.

> (G1: 72/OC3: 176)

Even if we grant that Rousseau's thought had grown in sophistication between the *Discourse on Inequality* and the *Social Contract*, so that the problem of inconsistency disappears, we may still be reluctant to agree with his claim that war conceptually implies a relationship between one *state* and another (and not between individuals) in the light of ethnic and civil strife in the Balkans, Rwanda and elsewhere. We could venture a reply on his behalf, though. Just as not every entity that calls itself a state is one in fact, there are many entities which exhibit state-like characteristics to the requisite degree while lacking that formal status. The Interhamwe of Rwanda that ordered the genocide of the Tutsis, and the Bosnian Serb political entity, each aspired to quite general authority over their ethnic communities (they claimed the right to command and the duty of obedience). We should note, though, that in other contexts, such as the state of pervasive conflict that immediately precedes the fraudulent social contract of the *Discourse on Inequality*, Rousseau is happy to use the term 'war' in a looser sense.

THE NEED FOR A FIRST CONVENTION (1.5)

Rousseau completes his discussion of possible alternatives to his own view in Book 1, Chapter 5. There, he tells us that there is all the difference in the world between a mere aggregation of individuals subject to a chief, and an association. An association is a genuine collective whose identity may outlive that of the particular individuals who compose it. Once again, Rousseau echoes Locke's discussion of the institution of civil society. For Locke, a tyranny was just another form of the state of nature, since the tyrant and his subjects were best seen as private individuals, bound by a relationship of force, who had no common judge to appeal to. Similarly, for Rousseau, a relationship between individuals subjected to a tyrant does not constitute a genuine political entity. He mentions again Grotius's view that a people might give themselves to a king. Such a view, he argues presupposes that the people are constituted as a people. What could constitute them as such? What could enable them to make collective decisions such as the institution of a monarch? What would decide the procedures, such as majority rule, according to which such a decision could be taken? All such things, Rousseau tells us, presuppose a prior convention.

Dialectically, Rousseau's purpose in 1.5 has been to prepare for his telling us what this convention will be like. We should note, though, that in the light of what is to follow in the *Social Contract*, he may have claimed too much. Certainly, later in the work, particularly when discussing the role of the lawgiver, Rousseau seems to presuppose that peoples can, after all, have some kind of collective existence and identity even before they give themselves a political form.

NOTES

1 For some modern discussions of legitimate state authority, see Wolff, *In Defense of Anarchism*; Simmons, *Moral Principles and Political Obligations*; and Raz, *The Morality of Freedom*. Here, I am assuming that what Simmons calls the correlativity thesis holds, namely, that if the state has the right to issue commands then subjects normally have a duty to obey.

2 At least, such is the claim made by Gildin in *Rousseau's Social Contract*, p. 18. Gildin derives the point from Leo Strauss but acknowledges that, as Derathé has pointed out, the allegedly Hobbesian reasoning is also present in Locke. Note also Rousseau's claim, in the third of the *Letters from the Mountain*, again noted by Gildin, that his treatment of these matters follows exactly the same principles as Locke (OC3: 812).

3 A useful exploration of Rousseau's developing attitude to Grotius and his wider role in the development of Rousseau's thought can be found in Roosevelt, *Reading Rousseau in the Nuclear Age*, especially ch. 2.

4 Grotius, *The Law of War and Peace*, III, 4 ix.

5 Aristotle, *Politics* 1252a.

6 For an especially brilliant exposition of this phenomenon, see Scott, *Domination and the Arts of Resistance*.

7 See Bales, 'The Social Psychology of Modern Slavery'. Bales writes:

> A... commonality among different forms of slavery is the psychological manipulation they all involve. The widely held conception of a slave is someone in chains who would escape if given half a chance or who simply does not know better. But ... this view is naive. In my experience, slaves often know that their enslavement is illegal. Force, violence and psychological coercion have convinced them to accept it. When slaves begin to accept their role and identify with their master, constant physical bondage becomes unnecessary. They come to perceive their situation not as a deliberate action taken to harm them in particular but as part of the normal, if regrettable, scheme of things.

8   E5: 358/OC4: 693. For extended discussion of Rousseau on relations between the sexes see O'Hagan, *Rousseau*, ch. 8.

9   Montesquieu, *Persian Letters*, p. 191.

10 Grotius, *The Law of War and Peace*, Book 1, III.8.

11 The editors of OC3 note Elie Luzac's objection that 'alienate' means more than just to give or sell but comprises any transfer of right (OC3: 1438).

12 Both Locke and Rousseau are, of course, being heavily ironic here. Ulysses did not passively accept the rule of the cyclops, but stabbed the beast in the eye with a huge poker and he and his men escaped from the cave fastened beneath the stomachs of sheep.

13 Montesquieu, *The Spirit of the Laws*, p. 236.

14 Steiner, *An Essay on Rights*, p. 232, n. 9.

15 Barbeyrac, 'Notes on Grotius', p. 373.

16 This important text had long been presented as an incoherent sequence of fragments until Grace G. Roosevelt worked out how to rearrange the parts to generate a consistent piece of writing. The story of how she did this is contained in the Introduction to her *Reading Rousseau in the Nuclear Age*. Her analysis of *The State of War* is contained at chs 2–3 of the same work.

17 See again Montesquieu's *Spirit of the Laws*, p. 236.

5

THE SOCIAL PACT AND PROPERTY

(Book 1, Chs 6–9)

Having eliminated various false ideas about political rule, the way is clear for Rousseau to begin to outline his own conception of what a legitimate political order looks like. He does this mainly in the two most compressed and closely articulated chapters of Book 1, Chapters 6 and 7. How does an aggregate of persons come to form a people? Why should they come together to form a state? What are the effects of them doing so?

> I assume men having reached the point where the obstacles that interfere with their preservation in the state of nature prevail by their resistance over the forces which each individual can muster to maintain himself in that state. Then that primitive state can no longer subsist, and humankind would perish if it did not change its way of being.
>
> (1.6.1)

This passage, and the ones that follow it, tell us something of the circumstances in which Rousseau envisages the social pact being enacted. The human beings who will construct a legitimate state are not human beings in a primitive state of nature. They are not the wood-wandering semi-humans of the *Discourse on Inequality*. Increase of population and technological development have brought human beings to a point where they can no longer satisfy their wants separately with little or no effect on one another. Rather, they are in a position where they are both interdependent and in a state of more or less endemic conflict and competition.

Rousseau has various differing accounts of the nature of this conflict, notably at the end of the *Discourse on Inequality* and in 'Of the General Society of the Human Race' in the *Geneva Manuscript*. In the published text of the *Social Contract* he does not make the nature of this immediately pre-political stage clear. In fact, Rousseau's picture appears to incorporate – in a somewhat unsatisfactory manner – aspects both of Hobbes's and of Locke's state of nature. So, for example, he tells us both that relations between individuals in this stage are mediated primarily by force with people enjoying something like a Hobbesian right of nature – with a 'right to everything that tempts him and he can reach' (1.8.2) *and* that the 'right of the first occupant' though 'so weak in the state of nature' (1.9.2) is nevertheless, when confirmed by labour and cultivation 'the only sign of property which others ought to respect in the absence of legal titles' (1.9.3). When we combine these remarks with those of the 'independent man' from the *Geneva Manuscript* who has a dim intimation of morality without being motivated to act justly, the picture we get is of a world where there is some appreciation of both self and others as actual or potential rights-bearers but where the individuals are subject to almost irresistible temptation to use force against others and are pressed by desperate circumstances into doing so.[1]

The central difficulty Rousseau believes he faces is how to form a social union that is consistent both with the individual's desire for self-preservation and with another characteristic that Rousseau has already told us about – his freedom. He has, after all, already emphasised that: 'To renounce one's freedom is to renounce one's quality as a man, the rights of humanity, and even its duties' (1.4.6). If our first duty is to preserve ourselves, how could it be consistent with that duty to submit to an authority that may limit one's individual pursuit of self-preservation? If freedom is they key morally defining characteristic of human beings, how could that be reconciled with a form of submission that may limit that very freedom?

Rousseau famously defines his task thus:

> To find a form of association that will defend and protect the person and goods of each associate with the full common force and by means of which each, uniting with all, nevertheless obeys only himself and remains as free as before.
>
> (1.6.4)

Rousseau's contention will be that the social contract, in establishing a form of society where all persons are subject to the general will, achieves precisely his aim of reconciling social order with individual freedom.

Having set out this programme, Rousseau tells us that the clauses of this social contract are 'so completely determined by the nature of the act that the slightest modification would make them null and void' (1.6.5). He also claims that they are everywhere the same and 'tacitly admitted and recognized'. It is far from clear exactly what he means by this. He surely cannot believe that in all societies the model of the social contract is actually implemented or observed. Rather, he must mean that the conditions of legitimacy embodied in the social contract are accessible and known to everyone at least to the point of paying lip service to them.[2]

Perhaps Rousseau's suggestion then, is that many existing institutions tacitly embody standards that the true social contract would realise. A thought along these lines *might* be justified. Many people have articulated the idea that Western liberal democracies fail to live up to the standards of freedom and equality before the law that they themselves proclaim. It would be rather surprising, though, if Rousseau were to suggest that the true standards of legitimacy are somehow recognised even in the most backward feudal regimes!

When he goes on to tell us what these clauses 'everywhere tacitly admitted and recognized' amount to, their allegedly universal acceptance becomes even more unlikely: '. . . the total alienation of each associate with all of his rights to the whole community' (1.6.6). More specifically:

> Each of us puts his person and his full power in common under the supreme direction of the general will; and in a body we receive each member as an indivisible part of the whole.
>
> (1.6.9)

It seems, on the face of things, outrageous that Rousseau should present this as a solution to the problem he posed earlier. How would such an alienation leave each as free as before? How does the absorption of the individual into a collective secure this freedom? How is my free government of myself compatible with being under the 'supreme direction' of the general will?

Recall, further, Rousseau's discussion of slavery by agreement in 1.4. There, he gives us an analysis of the word 'alienate' that he his now using and asks us what a people could possibly get in return for subjecting itself to a despot. He has just told us there that an agreement requiring 'absolute authority on one side, and unlimited obedience on the other, is vain and contradictory' (1.4.6), and that this contradictory nature nullifies the agreement itself.

As it turns out, Rousseau will argue that there is no contradiction here, even given the fact that in the social pact, the alienation is made 'without reservation'. First of all, he explains that since the renunciation is the same for all, no one has any interest in making it a burden for the rest. Second, he tells us that anything less than a total alienation would be no alienation at all, and would, rather, leave everyone in the state of nature. For, the retention of some right against the others or against the collective would leave the individual and his opponent in the situation of being judge in their own cause once the violation of that right was in question. Finally, he tells us – and repeats on a number of occasions – that there is no real loss involved in this act of renunciation – that one gains by the act more than one loses. As things stand, these are mere promissory notes by Rousseau that he has yet to make good on.

THE SOCIAL PACT

The social pact creates a new type of entity: 'a moral and collective body made up of as many members as the assembly has voices, and which receives by this same act its unity, its common *self*, its life and its will' (1.6.10). This collective has a number of names which correspond to its different *personae*, the most important of which, for us, is the name *Sovereign* which it has when an 'active' body. The persons who compose this sovereign and who have associated together to form it are 'citizens' when they are deliberating about the laws, and 'subjects' when they are subjected to them.

The details of Rousseau's social pact – which he presents somewhat obscurely – differ in important respects from other well-known examples in the social contract tradition. Rousseau explains at the beginning of 1.7 that the act of association involves each individual in a contract with *himself*. Compare this to Hobbes's account of 'commonwealth by institution' where 'every man' agrees with 'every man' that:

> I Authorise and give up my right of Governing my selfe, to this Man, or to this Assembly of men, on this condition, that thou give up thy Right to him, and Authorise all his Actions in like manner.[3]

Hobbes's individuals, then, neither contract with *themselves* to generate the sovereign, nor do they contract with the sovereign, but rather each contracts with each one of the others. Similarly, in Locke's *Second Treatise* individuals agree *with one another* to leave the state of nature and to create a political community. By contrast, it is slightly mysterious whom Rousseauian contractors contract with. They are clearly not making a series of bilateral promises on the Hobbesian model. Rousseau tells us that the sense in which a person contracts with himself involves a contract between himself under one description (natural man) and another (citizen). But to have the identity of citizen already *presupposes* the existence of the collective – you can't be a citizen until there is a citizen-body – so such a contract could not create it. Indeed, Rousseau sometimes expresses his idea as involving a contract between the individual and the public. As Robert Derathé has pointed out,[4] this is a difficulty of such a contract that is directly addressed by Hobbes in *De Cive*:

> Democracy is not framed by contract of particular persons with the *people*, but by mutual compacts of single men each with other. But hence it appears, in the first place, that the persons contracting must be in being before the contract itself. But the *people* is not in being before the constitution of government, as not being any person, but a multitude of single persons; wherefore there could then no contract pass between the people and the subject.
>
> (*De Cive*, 7, 7)

Unlike Hobbes, Rousseau is prepared to indulge in a *fiction*, namely that the sovereign people already have a virtual existence at the moment of the agreement that generates them as a collective. The agreement that creates the public power is an agreement between individuals and that very public. The temporal and logical problems posed by this contract are matched by another severe difficulty which Rousseau does not clearly express in the *Social Contract* itself, but makes explicit in his summary statement in *Emile*:

> Since the two contracting parties – that is, each individual and the public – have no common superior who can judge their differences, we shall examine whether each party remains the master of breaking the contract when it pleases him – that is to say, of renouncing it as soon as he believes himself injured.
>
> (E5: 461/OC4: 840)

It is *this* problem – the problem of who is to judge when the pact is broken – that is the focus of Rousseau's otherwise slightly cryptic passage at 1.7.5–7. Rousseau solves it conceptually by arguing that since the sovereign's power is made up of the people themselves it simply *could not be* that the sovereign would act in a way that violates the fundamental agreement. By contrast, he suggests that individuals as subjects may be all too easily tempted to act in an agreement-violating way. Consequently, while citizens have no need of an impartial judge or common superior to ensure sovereign compliance with the social pact and have no right individually to judge that the social pact has been broken, the sovereign 'must find means to ensure [the] fidelity' of individuals as subjects (1.7.6).

Rousseau's argument here, that the sovereign cannot harm individual citizens, is both extremely unsatisfactory and – given that it relies on matters that he has yet to discuss, such as the character of the general will – rather opaque. Rousseau's basic suggestion is that since citizens are themselves the authors of the laws that they are subject to, they could have no reason to legislate oppressively. Unlike in Hobbes's system, where subjects are formally deemed to be the authors of the sovereign's actions, in Rousseau's argument citizens, collectively, really do will the law. As Rousseau will come to explain in Book 2, the form in which the sovereign's commands must be expressed, that of general and universally applicable laws, provides a reason for believing that in a well-constituted state the sovereign will not act tyrannically. But not only are these arguments yet to come, and objections to them yet to be met, it is not even clear how *relevant* they are in this context. Here, Rousseau writes:

> Now the Sovereign, since it is formed entirely of the individuals who make it up, has not, and cannot have any interests contrary to theirs; consequently the Sovereign power has no need of a guarantor towards the subjects, because it is impossible for the body to want to harm all of its members, and we shall see later that it cannot harm any one of them in particular. The Sovereign, by the mere fact that it is, is always everything it ought to be.
>
> (1.7.5)

But there are plainly at least three acute difficulties here: majority rule, intrusive and paternalistic opinions among the citizenry, and the problem of determining when the sovereign 'is' (that is, when the people are acting legitimately as a sovereign body). The first difficulty, that of majority rule, is one that Rousseau believes he will solve later. The general will cannot, he believes, by the form it takes and the manner in which it is expressed, become the tool by which majorities impose their selfish interests on minorities. The second problem, which he never considers, concerns not people's selfish pursuit of their interests but, rather, moral views which they try to promote using the public power, for what are, by their own lights, altruistic reasons. If a majority of the population believes, for example, that homosexuality leads to damnation, they may well use the public power to save gays from themselves. The advocates of such a proposal would not want to harm any of their fellow citizens, but that is what they would be doing.[5] The third difficulty, though, is the one that is most acute at this point. Rousseau is, here, rejecting the idea that individuals might, in the absence of a common superior, retain the right to judge whether or not the social pact has been broken by the sovereign. It is no answer at all to say that so long as the sovereign retains the characteristics of sovereignty then its breaking of the social pact is conceptually excluded. As we shall see, much of Book 3 of the *Social Contract* is devoted to tracing the ways in which the sovereign power can degenerate or be usurped. When a corrupted citizenry yields effective control of the state to a plutocratic faction, the sovereign, in the strict sense of the word, no longer exists and the social pact is broken. But those who then wield state power will no doubt continue to *claim* that sovereign power exists: Rousseau wants to deny the citizen the right to judge whether the sovereign has broken the social pact, but he must in such circumstances allow the individual the right to judge whether the sovereign *is*.[6]

While Rousseau is supremely and unwarrantedly optimistic that the sovereign will not, in fact, pursue interests contrary to those of the individuals composing it, he does think that there is a grave danger of individuals pursuing particular interests contrary to those of the collective:

> . . . each individual may, as a man, have a particular will contrary to or different from the general will he has as a Citizen. His particular interest may speak to him quite differently from the common interest; his absolute and naturally independent existence may lead him to look upon what he owes to the common cause as a gratuitous

contribution, the loss of which will harm others less than its payment burdens him and, by considering the moral person that constitutes the State as a being of reason because it is not a man, he would enjoy the rights of a citizen without being willing to fulfil the duties of a subject; an injustice, the progress of which would cause the ruin of the body politic.

(1.7.7)

One way of understanding this paragraph is as a brilliantly clear and compressed statement of the problem of public goods and collective action. The problem is this: all collectively, and each individually, stand to benefit from the provision of some good, such as the provision of social order by a framework of law. Yet each person also knows that whether the good in question will continue to be provided does not depend on their personal contribution. Accordingly, each individual – motivated by a sense of his 'absolute and naturally independent existence' – will be tempted to try to get the benefit while exempting themselves from the cost. Each may attempt to enjoy the social peace provided by the legal system while avoiding complying with the law themselves. The danger here is of a domino effect. Citizens who perceive their fellows enjoying 'the rights of a citizen' while getting away with not fulfilling the 'duties of a subject' will be tempted to act likewise, and this will lead eventually to the 'ruin of the body politic'.

Chapter 7 concludes with Rousseau's famous (or notorious) passage explaining that when citizens are constrained to obey the general will, they are thereby forced to be free. It will be helpful to postpone the elucidation of those words until we have had a chance to look at the transformation in the human condition that Rousseau claims the social pact brings about and at his remarks on the nature of freedom.

THE 'REMARKABLE CHANGE IN MAN' (1.8)

One of the most striking differences between Rousseau and other contractarians such as Hobbes and Locke is in his contention that the act of association produces a fundamental change in the nature of the associates. Whereas both Hobbes and Locke justify the contract in terms of the antecedent interests of the participants – with Hobbes showing us how acquisitive and short-sighted individuals are led by the desire to preserve themselves to submit to an absolute sovereign who changes the incentive structure facing them, and Locke telling us a story about how people institute civil government for the preservation of their 'lives, liberties and estates' – Rousseauian individuals are themselves transformed by the process of association. Rousseau sets this idea out in typically eloquent and powerful style at the beginning of 1.8:

> This transition from the state of nature to the civil state produces a most remarkable change in man by substituting justice for instinct in his conduct, and endowing his actions with the morality they previously lacked. Only then, when the voice of duty succeeds physical impulsion and right succeeds appetite, does man, who until then had looked only to himself, see himself forced to act on other principles, and to consult his reason before listening to his inclinations. Although in this state he deprives himself of several advantages he has from nature, he gains such great advantages in return, his faculties are exercised and developed, his ideas enlarged, his sentiments ennobled, his entire soul is elevated to such an extent, that if the abuses of the new condition did not often degrade him to beneath the condition he has left, he should ceaselessly bless the happy moment which wrested him from it forever, and out of a stupid and bounded animal made an intelligent being and a man.
>
> (1.8.1)

On a hasty reading this passage, with its positive moral evaluation of the civil state compared to the primitive state, might be thought to be in contradiction with the message of the first two *Discourses*. But, in fact, Rousseau is careful to distinguish between the moral *possibilities* of the transition from the state of nature and the all too frequent actuality. He is suggesting that if a genuinely well-ordered state is brought into being, it offers human beings, for the first time, the opportunity for genuinely moral action. The passage is also significant, together with the chapter of which it forms a part, in seeking to draw up a balance sheet setting out the gains and losses of the transition.

Here, Rousseau's focus is on human nature and he draws a series of contrasts between man in the state of nature and man in the civil state. In the state of nature, man is guided by instinct or physical impulsion or inclination; in the civil state, the directing principles are justice and reason. In the one he is a 'stupid and bounded animal' and in the other 'an intelligent being and a man'. The whole passage strongly calls to mind others, particularly in Chapter 2 of the *Geneva Manuscript* that also draw the contrast between a limited animal existence and one guided by reason and morality. Rousseau's thought here is that artifice, in the shape of new institutions, can direct and modify human nature so that citizens take account of the existence of personhood of others in pursuing their own interests. Whereas instinct, in the shape of *amour de soi* and *pitié* ensured the peaceful coexistence of animal-humans in the primitive state of nature, reason and conscience can do the same in the civil state, so long as *amour propre* is properly managed and controlled. If it is not, of course, the 'abuses of this new condition' will 'often degrade him beneath the condition he has left'.

The passage about the 'remarkable change' does raise a difficulty for a theory that advertises itself as 'contractarian'. In a contractarian theory of state legitimacy it is reasonable to suppose that the fact of agreement will play an important normative role: that one reason that people ought to obey the law is that they agreed to the social pact. In hypothetical versions of the contract, we might highlight the fact that people *would have agreed*. But if the creation of the civil state does, indeed, bring about a 'remarkable change', it is at least arguable that the contractors will no longer recognise themselves in the persons who agreed (or who would have agreed) to the social pact. Indeed, it may turn out that the transformed persons have quite different reasons for allegiance to the state than the original contractors.

FREEDOM

We have already seen Rousseau make use of the notion of freedom in his opening lines – 'Man is born free . . .' – and in his rejection

THE SOCIAL PACT AND PROPERTY

of slavery. Now we need to say a little more about his understanding of the concept in order to illuminate what is to come. Modern discussion of freedom has centred around the contrast between so-called 'negative' and 'positive' freedom. Negative libertarianism understands freedom or liberty as an absence of constraint; positive libertarianism focuses on an agent's achievement of self-rule or autonomy. For a positive libertarian, freedom is a matter not simply (or not even) of being unconstrained but rather of making it so as people act on the best reasons that apply to them. Sometimes critics of positive libertarianism suggest that an agent who is constrained to act on the most applicable reasons is, by positive libertarian lights, forced to act freely even where that agent does not understand or acknowledge those applicable reasons. This is, it is suggested, an absurd consequence of the positive libertarian view.

Hostile commentators often see Rousseau as being the theorist of positive liberty par excellence. And indeed, as we shall see, there are certainly passages in the *Social Contract* which suggest such a reading. But taking the book as a whole, together with Rousseau's other writings, such an understanding of his thought is most one-sided and fails to do justice to the subtlety and complexity of his view. When considering this issue, we should always keep in mind the great aim of the *Social Contract*: to find a 'form of association' in which each person remains as 'free as before' (1.6.4). Any plausible and attractive reading of Rousseau's text should have him understanding freedom in such a way as to make whatever answers to this aim both successful in its own terms and at least possessing a prima facie plausibility for us, his readers.

In the *Social Contract*, although Rousseau distinguishes among types of freedom, he neglects to give a general characterisation of freedom as such. We can, however, draw on his remarks elsewhere, most notably in the *Letters from the Mountain*. There he writes:

> Liberty consists less in doing one's will than in not being subject to that of another; it consists also in not submitting the will of another to our own, Whoever is master cannot be free and to reign is to obey.

> (OC3: 841)

This sits very well with his statement at the very beginning of the *Social Contract* that one who 'believes himself the other's master . . . yet is more a slave than they' (1.1.1). Freedom, then, is most basically a matter of not being subject to the command or domination of particular other people, not being subject to their capricious whims. The law, by establishing a conventional relationship among citizens that treats them as equals, frees them from the relations of force and opinion that would otherwise hold sway. In his insistence that freedom involves not being subject to the whims of others, Rousseau again echoes Locke whose characterisation of man's natural state involves just such non-subjection, it is 'a State of perfect Freedom to order their Actions and dispose of their Possessions, and Persons, as they think fit, within the bounds of the Law of Nature, without asking leave or depending upon the Will of any other Man' (*Second Treatise*: §4).

Where Rousseau differs from Locke, of course, is in his much broader construal of the ways in which a person's will may become subject to the will of another. Whereas, for Locke, the guarantee of certain basic rights (together with a system of impartial justice) gives each person a domain that is protected from the encroachment of others, Rousseau foresees the possibility of such encroachment even if such a system of rights is in place.

This, indeed, is the message that Rousseau wants us to take from the fraudulent social contract that he explored in the final pages of his *Discourse on Inequality*. Rousseau believes that a system of individual rights of private property and self-ownership that is accompanied by massive disparities of wealth and income inevitably leads to distortion and deformation of the will as people seek to curry favour or seek advantage. A crucial difference between the two, though, is this: that whereas Locke takes individual rights to be clearly established prior to, and outside of, the construction of any particular political community and sees overweening state power as being the principal threat to individual liberty, Rousseau sees the state as the principal source and guarantor of citizen's rights and sees the main threat to individual freedom as being inequality and corruption in civil society which, if unchecked, will lead to the capture of the public power by private interests. The state is justified by the fact that the association is needed to secure the liberty of individuals but the public person has to regulate that very liberty to preserve it.

At 1.8.2–3 of the *Social Contract*, Rousseau distinguishes three types of freedom. First, he mentions 'natural freedom'. He tells us associates lose their natural freedom when they associate to become citizens. This loss of natural freedom which 'has no other bounds than the individual's forces', means the forfeiture of 'an unlimited right to everything that tempts him and he can reach' (1.8.2). Individuals in a state of nature had only been limited in achieving their goals by physical constraints, including the physical power and presence of other humans (and animals). The liberty they enjoyed in that state implied no duty towards individuals or from others to them. In such a condition their relationship to external objects and land is one of mere physical possession.

Second, Rousseau refers to 'civil freedom and property in everything he possesses'. Unlike natural freedom, civil freedom is 'limited by the general will' and is accompanied by a new way of relating to external objects: *property*. While a person's natural freedom was limited only by *physical* factors, their *civil* freedom involves an ineliminable reference to other persons. The rights people have under conditions of civil liberty are properly understood as rights that imply duties on the part of others. Citizens no longer have a right to all things, but only a right to those things and actions that are properly theirs, a right that is limited by the right that others have to their things, persons and actions. Rousseau tells us that in entering the civil state, we lose our 'natural' freedom and gain this 'civil' freedom (1.8.2). The motive for making this exchange is set out clearly by Hobbes, who remarks on the practical worthlessness of 'natural' freedom:

> But it was the least benefit for men thus to have a common right to all things. For the effects of this right are the same, almost, as if there had been no right at all. For although any man may say of every thing, *this is mine*, yet he could not enjoy it, by reason of his neighbour,

who having equal right and equal power, would pretend the same thing to be his.

(De Cive, 1, 11)

Given the manifest defects of the state of nature, Hobbes tells us that the law of nature (a rule of reason telling us what is conducive to our mutual preservation) requires that each person be willing '*to lay down this right to all things; and be contented with so much liberty against other men, as he would allow other men against himselfe*' (*Leviathan*, ch. 14, p. 92, emphasis in original). Right reason dictates that we give up a liberty unconstrained by anything other than physical force in favour of a reasonable recognition that one's own liberty should be limited by the similar liberty of others. Do persons bound by such a regime of mutual recognition of one another's rights enjoy *liberty*? A full answer to that question may yet depend on a setting out of what, exactly, the rights they enjoy are. But, at least on the face of things, in insisting on the need for liberty to be limited for the sake of liberty, Rousseau has said nothing that a libertarian need take exception to.

What might raise libertarian concern is his insistence that this civil freedom is 'limited by the general will' (1.8.2). Until we have a clear idea of what the general will is and what its content might be, there has to be a concern that the public power will impose severe restrictions on the size of domains within which individuals have discretion to act. Rousseau will argue, successfully or not, that the sovereign people can have no interest in acting intrusively or oppressively. In allowing the collective to set the content of individuals' rights, though, Rousseau clearly envisages a more interventionist state than Locke did. But on Rousseau's view, as we shall see, regulation of individual freedom so as to do things like maintain a rough material equality is not only permissible but, indeed, required if individuals are not to become subject to the particular wills of others.

The third type of freedom Rousseau mentions at 1.8 is what he calls 'moral freedom'. This type of freedom he characterises as 'obedience to the law one has prescribed to oneself'. He contrasts this type of action with the 'impulsion of mere appetite' (1.8.3).

Rousseau presents this third type of freedom as a kind of added bonus of the civil state, rather than being its goal. Certainly it forms no part of the citizens' reasons for associating together in the first place, since it is a benefit they cannot yet see. Their reasons for associating have to be expressed in terms of the securing of their survival while escaping from personal subjection (1.8.3).

But, though 'moral freedom' may not figure in the motives of the first associates it clearly has significance for the programme which Rousseau enunciated at 1.6.4 where he insisted that each person, within a properly constituted civil state would 'obey only himself and remain as free as before', although it is far from clear, from Rousseau's formulation there what he intends the relationship between obedience to self and freedom to be. We might read the formula in at least three ways: (1) each person obeys only himself and *also* remains as free as before; (2) each person obeys only himself and, *that is to say*, remains as free as before; and (3) each person obeys only himself and *thereby* or *by this means* remains as free as before. Moreover, we could understand the 'as free as' clause to mean as *naturally*, as *civilly* or as *morally* free as before.

Later in the *Social Contract*, Rousseau will seek to rely on the claim that each individual wills the general will in order to argue that obedience to that general will is not a restriction on their freedom. He will certainly want to claim, also, that obedience to the general will enables people to secure their true interests. But the content that he gives to those true interests brings us back sharply to his notion of freedom as non-subjection to the will of particular others. Submitting to a regime of equality before the law enables us to secure our critical interest in not being subjected (or so Rousseau would claim). The connection comes out when we turn back to the notorious words at the end of 1.7:

> Hence for the social compact not to be an empty formula, it tacitly includes the following engagement which alone can give force to the rest, that whoever refuses to obey the general will shall be constrained to do so by the entire body: which means nothing other than that he shall be forced to be free . . .
>
> (1.7.8)

But these alarming and typically paradoxical words are immediately followed by: 'for this is the condition which, by giving each Citizen to the Fatherland, guarantees him against all personal dependence'.

The citizen is guaranteed a right to equal freedom by the general will, but this right necessarily implies constraint, so that one person's freedom is compatible with that of all others. When other thinkers have expressed the same thought, in very similar terms, they have not been understood as issuing an apologia for tyranny. So, for example, Kant, in the *Metaphysical Elements of Justice*, having formulated as the universal principle of justice that: 'Every action is just that in itself or in its maxim is such that the freedom of the will of each can coexist with the freedom of everyone in accordance with a universal law', continues by explaining that:

> if a certain use of freedom is itself a hindrance to freedom according to universal laws, . . . then the use of coercion to counteract it, inasmuch as it is the prevention of a hindrance to freedom, is consistent with freedom according to universal laws; in other words, this use of coercion is just.[7]

So, there are two strings to Rousseau's bow here. The first is that the general will guarantees a right to equal freedom and, hence, ensures that no individual becomes subject to the command of any other individual. The second is that insofar as the public power is wielded against individuals in the form of general regulations or laws limiting property rights, it is essential that this public power genuinely belongs to everyone: that it be mine as much as yours. If, in obeying the general will, I were, in fact, subject to the particular selfish will of some other person or group of persons, then I would be unfree. Much of the rest of the *Social Contract* is devoted to explaining the nature of sovereignty and the general will and the contrast between particular and general wills, so it would be wrong to anticipate here whether Rousseau succeeds in his claim that the general will is necessarily non-oppressive. His basic thesis, that the general will is compatible with (indeed embodies) freedom, is well set out in the following unpublished fragment:

> One is free, although subject to laws, and not when one obeys a
> man, because in the latter case I obey the will of another but in
> obeying the Law I only obey the public will which is as much mine
> as it is anyone else's. Besides, a master can permit to one person
> something that he prohibits to another, whereas the law, in making
> no exceptions renders equal the condition of all and in consequence
> there is neither master nor servant.[8]

In obeying the law, I obey a will that is my own and which ensures
that I am subject to the same restrictions as anyone else. My right
to equal freedom with all other private persons is guaranteed.

PROPERTY (1.9)

Rousseau's attitude to private property appears to shift a great deal
over his various writings. In the *Discourse on Inequality*, where he
is broadly hostile to its claims, property has its origin in agriculture. People need the assurance that the land they have worked on
(by ploughing and sowing seeds) will not be taken from them before
they can harvest their crops. In the conjectural history contained in
that work, the idea of property once it had taken hold, combined
with natural inequalities, luck and the passing on of farms from one
generation to the next to generate dependence and social division,
Rousseau spells out the consequences:

> . . . once inheritances had increased in number and size to the point
> where they covered all the land and all adjoined one another, men
> could no longer aggrandize themselves except at one another's
> expense, and the supernumaries whom weakness or indolence had
> kept from acquiring an inheritance of their own . . . were obliged to
> receive or seize their subsistence from the hands of the rich . . .
>
> (G1: 171/OC3: 175)

Understandably, the dispossessed were less than happy to accept
their exclusion and claimed 'on the basis of their strength or of their
needs, a kind of right to another person's good, equivalent, according
to them, to the right of property' (G1: 171/OC3: 176). Nor was
there any effective reply to their claim, since:

Even those whom industriousness alone had enriched could scarcely base their property on better titles. No matter if they said: It is I who built this wall; I earned this plot by my labour. Who set its boundaries for you, they could be answered; and by virtue of what do you lay claim to being paid at our expense for labor we did not impose on you? Do you not know that a great many of your brothers perish or suffer from need of what you have in excess, and that you required the express and unanimous consent of Humankind to appropriate for yourself anything from the common subsistence above and beyond your own?

(G1: 172/OC3: 176)

The message of the *Discourse on Inequality*, then, is that although labour does convey a title to property on the basis of the effort put in by the individual, that title is always a provisional one in the state of nature. Since there can be other claims to the same piece of land with a normative basis that is at least as good, there is a foundation for irreconcilable conflict and, indeed, Rousseau there gives such conflict as one of the major causes of the descent into something approaching the Hobbesian state of war.

In other writings, such as the *Discourse on Political Economy* and the *Constitutional Project for Corsica*, Rousseau addresses himself not to the origins of property claims in a state of nature, but the role and nature of property in civil society. In *Political Economy* he adopts a highly favourable tone:

It is certain that the right of property is the most sacred of all the rights of citizens, and more important in some respects than freedom itself; either because it bears more directly on the preservation of life; or because goods being easier to usurp and more difficult to defend than persons, greater respect ought to be accorded to what can more easily be seized; or, finally, because property is the true foundation of civil society; and the true guarantee of citizens' commitments: for if persons were not answerable with their goods, nothing would be so easy as to elude one's duties and scoff at the laws.

(G2: 23/OC3: 263)

But even at his most enthusiastic, Rousseau stops well short of endorsing an absolutist conception of private property. Rather, he sees the state as entitled to raise taxation and to modify the various 'incidents' of property, especially by regulating wills, inheritances and contracts. He argues that in order to defend the rights of private property, the state must be granted the means to do so and that this inevitably requires modification to the right of private property itself. In sharp contrast to his statements in *Political Economy*, in the *Constitutional Project for Corsica* he endorses a much more collectivist view than we find elsewhere in his writings:

> Far from wanting the state to be poor, I should like, on the contrary for it to own everything, and for the individual to share in the common property only in proportion to his services ... In short, I want the property of the state to be as large and strong, that of the citizens as small and weak as possible.[9]

The discussion in the *Social Contract* is perhaps best thought of as taking a middle course between *Political Economy* and *Corsica*. Rousseau broadly endorses private property within the civil state, but is prepared for the sovereign to intervene where necessary to rein in property in the interest of equality and civic unity.

The fact that Rousseau places his discussion 'Of Real Property' immediately after his discussion of the various types of freedom is significant. It suggests that he thinks of the nature and extent of individual property-holding as being a central component of the civil liberty they enjoy. In this chapter, Rousseau's discussion sometimes recalls Locke's in the *Second Treatise of Government*. Nevertheless, there are two crucial differences from Locke's account. First, whereas for Locke, fully fledged rights of private property can come into being in the state of nature, for Rousseau this only happens with the establishment of a political community via the social pact. Second, Locke is very quick to depart from his initial limitations on acquisition, while Rousseau maintains a very strict limit on the extent of legitimate appropriation.

Rousseau begins his account by repeating that the social pact involves the total alienation of individuals with all their goods to the community. But he explains that, though this is, as it were, the legal form of things, what is actually happening is that mere possession is being underwritten by the state and is being turned into private property. This creates a somewhat paradoxical situation: within the state, individuals owe their claim on their holdings to positive law. If questions are raised as to a citizen's right to occupy and work a piece of land, they are appropriately answered by reference to legal title. But though the claims and disputes among citizens are to be settled by reference to law, the claim of the state over its territory cannot be settled in the same manner. With respect to outsiders and other political communities, the state is like a private person. It shares no common judge or framework of law to underwrite its territorial claims or to resolve disputes. Accordingly, Rousseau says, the right it possesses over its territory is the 'right of the first occupant' which it derives from the private individuals who have contracted together to form the state.

Rousseau's discussion of the right of the first occupant is quite compressed and perfunctory. Nevertheless, it raises some difficulties for the rather neat schema that Rousseau has used to describe the transition from the state of nature to the civil state. In his earlier discussion, he had contrasted natural liberty with civil liberty and mere possession with property. But it is clear from his account of the right of the first occupant that possession is, or at any rate can or ought to be, something morally more substantial than the kind of possession intended by a Hobbesian liberty to use everything. At 1.9.2 he tells us that 'The right of the first occupant, although more real than the right of the stronger, becomes a true right only after the right of property has been established'. And at 1.9.3 he sets out the conditions for making the right of the first occupant effective and, having told us that land must be previously un-inhabited and that appropriation is limited to what is needful for subsistence, he argues that appropriators must 'take possession of it not by a vain ceremony, but by labour and cultivation, the only sign of property which others ought to respect in the absence of legal titles'. So he is arguing that, even before a political community and legal framework is established, people can achieve a claim right over land that others have a duty to respect. This right has a greater 'reality' than mere force – which, as we have seen gives no right at all. In *Emile*, Rousseau argues in a similar way that the idea of property 'naturally goes back to the right of the first occupant by labour' (E2: 99/OC4: 332–3), when he discusses inculcating the idea of property into a child by getting him to plant a row of beans. He has the child Emile plant the beans where the gardener Robert has already planted some melons. The violation of antecedent property right and the associated sentiment of injustice are used by Rousseau to get across the notion of reciprocal respect of one another's rights. If nothing else, these passages should dispel the idea that Rousseau takes a purely Hobbesian view of binding norms in the state of nature, an idea that might be grounded in a hasty reading of his debate with Diderot. However tenuous their nature, he clearly believes that rights over land that one has a moral reason to respect can be justly established in a state of nature. He is clear, though, that the right of the first occupant is strictly circumscribed by need. In both the *Social Contract* and *Emile* he ridicules the idea that a person might, simply by declaration, seize control of a large territory.

In stressing labour as providing title to land Rousseau is following Locke. But whereas Locke's emphasis is on the way in which a person's ownership through labour excludes the common right of *others*, Rousseau stresses that once someone has privatised a piece of the common for their own benefit they thereby exclude *themselves* from the common. By this he must mean not that they are excluded from *all* use of the common land, but rather that they, having opted to subsist by farming a restricted area must not make use of common resources for their subsistence where other non-privatisers need that land for hunting and gathering. So, though Locke and Rousseau each limit the right of ownership by a proviso stipulating that one can take no more than one can make use of, Rousseau is even more restrictive than Locke was.[10]

The relationship between individual holdings and the state is dealt with in three paragraphs at 1.9.5–8. Rousseau clearly states that parcels of property are held by individuals as trustees for the public good and that 'the right every individual has over his land is always subordinate to the right the community has over everyone'.

He claims that this is, in fact, to the advantage of the property holder, since the public power with an interest in the land now secures individuals against the action both of their fellow citizens and of foreign invaders. Of course, the worry that many of Rousseau's readers will have is that while the state may indeed protect individuals against one another, what is to protect them against the state? Implicitly, Rousseau's answer has to be that the general will always takes the form of law and law is, by its very nature, not directed to particular objects but to general ones. But that answer is yet to be elaborated (it comes in Book 2). Here, he says little, although he is a little more expansive in a paragraph from the summary of the *Social Contract* in *Emile*. There he explains that:

> ... the sovereign has no right to touch the possessions of one or more individuals. But it can legitimately seize the possessions of all, as was done at Sparta in the time of Lycurgus; the abolition of debts by Solon, on the other hand, was an illegitimate act.
>
> (E5: 461–2/OC4: 841)

This does not, though, shed a great deal of light on the matter. Lycurgus's decree, just as much as Solon's, harmed the rich and assisted the poor. However, it did not do so by intervening in the bilateral relationships among citizens. This hardly seems to be a difference of sufficient significance to afford citizens protection.

Rousseau ends the first book with a summary paragraph and a footnote which, together, both clarify what has gone before and point to what is to come. The social pact, he tells us, replaces relations between citizens that are based on force with a new set of relations based on law. Whether or not people may be said to have a natural right to equal freedom, they do not actually enjoy such a right in the pre-political state where the right of the stronger prevails. In the civil state, however, such a right is positively established by law in the interests of all. But Rousseau is alive to the way in which the *pays legal* may not be an accurate guide to the *pays réel*. A legal equality among men that simply vests them all with the same abstract rights of citizenship will not establish or protect genuinely equal freedom if there are wide inequalities in the holdings of private property. Rousseau believes that it is essential that the sovereign power is used to ensure a dispersal of holdings such that all have sufficient property for their needs and none have too much. If substantial material inequality were to take hold then people would no longer enjoy the independence from the particular wills of others that Rousseau takes to be constitutive of their freedom.

NOTES

1   On this reading, Rousseau does believe that the precepts of something like Lockean natural law are morally binding in a state of anarchy, but the conditions under which such precepts would be widely respected are not met. This is, needless to say, a controversial view and others emphasise the more Hobbesian strands in Rousseau's position. We shall return to this question presently when we consider Rousseau's discussion 'Of Real Property' at 1.9.

2   In this respect, Rousseau's remarks are reminiscent of Diderot's article 'Natural Right' that he had himself challenged in the second chapter of the *Geneva Manuscript*. There, Diderot had asked where the general will was to be found and answered:

> In the principles and prescribed law of all civilised nations; in the social practices of savage and barbarous peoples; in the tacit agreements obtaining amongst the enemies of mankind; and even in those two emotions – indignation and resentment – which nature has extended as far as animals to compensate for social laws and public retribution.
>
> (*Political Writings*, p. 20)

3   Hobbes, *Leviathan* (1651), p. 120 [87].
4   See Derathé, *Jean-Jacques Rousseau et La Science Politique de son Temps*, p. 223.
5   As C. S. Lewis puts it:

> Of all tyrannies a tyranny sincerely exercised for the good of its victims may be the most oppressive. It may be better to live under robber barons than under omnipotent moral busybodies.

> The robber baron's cruelty may sometimes sleep, his cupidity may at some point be satiated; but those who torment us for own good will torment us without end, for they do so with the approval of their own conscience.
>
> ('The Humanitarian Theory of Punishment', p. 292)

6 It might be thought here that I am ignoring the distinction between the sovereign people and the government. I am not. My comments concern the case where the people continue to assemble and to conform, formally, with what sovereignty requires, but where something like a combination of apathy and bribery mean that real power is in the hands of a minority. As I mention below, in Chapter 8, such reserved rights to judge whether the sovereign still 'is' cannot form part of the constitution for reasons Kant explores but Rousseau does not.

7 Kant, *The Metaphysical Elements of Justice*, pp. 35–6.

8 *Fragments Politiques*, in OC3: 492.

9 OC3: 930–1 (translation from Hope Mason, *The Indispensable Rousseau*, p. 273). Hope Mason points out in a footnote that Rousseau was opposed to retrospective legislation, so Rousseau's collectivist aim would have had to be pursued without despoiling citizens of land they already possessed.

10 Locke, notoriously, suspends his limitation on acquisition as soon as the conventional device of money has been invented.

6

SOVEREIGNTY AND
THE GENERAL WILL

(Book 2, Chs 1–6)

In a letter to Marcet de Mézières of 24 July 1762, Rousseau states that the principles of government established in the *Social Contract* can be reduced to just two: 'The first, that legitimately sovereignty always belongs to the people; the second, that aristocracy is the best of all forms of government'.[1] Book 2 centres on the first of these principles, and Book 3 on the second. It is the people who are to exercise supreme power in the state rather than kings, tyrants or even parliaments. In fact, sovereignty is nothing but the exercise of the general will of the people, or, more exactly, the direction of the common force of the united citizenry by principles that issue from their general will.

All of this raises the question of what Rousseau means by the 'general will'. Here, many readers have found Rousseau's account confusing. One reason for this is the poorly integrated nature of his text. We have, in effect, to piece together a systematic account of the general will from various scattered references to it in the text. And when we look at what Rousseau writes *about* the general will we are likely to find ourselves pulled in conflicting interpretative directions. Sometimes the general will seems to mean little more than the decisions actually taken by the assembled citizen body. In other places, Rousseau tells us that this assembly can make mistakes, can fail to decide according to the general will, and that even when the state is corrupt and all but dissolved, the general will persists, as pure as it ever was.

We have, then, at least two, apparently contradictory, conceptions of the general will: the general will as *decision* and the general will as a *transcendent standard or principle*. Further adding to the complexity of this picture is the fact that Rousseau writes of the general will not only as an attribute of the people as a whole, but also as a property of each individual. In this chapter I look at what Rousseau has to say in the first part of Book 2 about the nature of the sovereign, but I also draw on both earlier and later chapters of the *Social Contract*. In doing so I have regard to Rousseau's larger project as programmatically stated at 1.6.4: a society governed by the general will must, in some plausible sense leave the associates as free as they were before and obeying only themselves. I argue that Rousseau believes that, given a context of sufficient social homogeneity and material equality, if the sovereign assembly is properly constituted and its procedures are properly followed it will be a fallible, but normally reliable mechanism for determining where the common good lies. Both collectively and individually citizens have an interest in the promotion of their common good, for only through it can their most vital interest in survival and freedom be guaranteed. Since they 'will' whatever conduces to the securing of their most vital interests and the sovereign assembly is a fallible but normally reliable indicator of what answers to that need, they will the outcome of collective deliberation even in those cases where they are in a minority. Where the democratic mechanism functions properly, then, the state is governed according to the general will. Where the process misfires and the common good is not pursued, the citizens continue to will the general will, but there is no way of ascertaining its content and popular sovereignty fails.

EARLIER MENTIONS OF THE GENERAL WILL

By the time we come to Book 2 we have already encountered the concept of the general will at 1.7.7–8. In that passage, we learnt that the general will concerns the common interest of the citizens, and that it contrasts with the particular interest of each member of the community. We also discovered that each person wills the general will in their *role* as citizen, and that all stand to benefit from co-operating together in the common interest but that there is a potential free-rider problem that might lead to opportunistic selfishness and that this must be avoided. We also know, from Chapter 2 of the *Geneva Manuscript*, that Rousseau there mentions a quite different conception of the general will, Diderot's 'general will of the human race', a conception Rousseau rejects as inadequate for peaceful and fruitful co-operation. Like Rousseau's general will, Diderot's idea is associated with a common interest (that of the totality of human beings) and with a description (that of the human being *as such*). But Rousseau argues that Diderot's notion has insufficient motivational grip to surmount the temptations to aggression and exploitation that individuals face. This naturally suggests that he believes that his own conception of the general will, that of a *particular* society, will be able to overcome and subsume such difficulties. The general will, then, is not general with respect to human beings as such, but has to do with the common interest of the members of a particular political community.

THE INALIENABILITY AND INDIVISIBILITY OF SOVEREIGNTY (2.1–2)

Rousseau opens Book 2 with two chapters arguing that sovereignty is 'inalienable' and 'indivisible'. His main purpose here is to reject the idea that sovereignty could be exercised by someone other than the people as a whole and yet still count as their rule. Sovereignty, for Rousseau, is a matter of the people applying their capacity for deliberation and decision to the direction of the state, just as autonomous action by an individual involves the application of *their* capacity for deliberation and decision to what they do. Rousseau wants to say that in the collective case, as in the individual one, it makes no sense to say, in cases where person A always or generally decides for person B, that the resulting action be nevertheless attributed to B. In taking this stance he is particularly concerned to rebut the Hobbesian view that the people might grant someone other than themselves absolute authority to act on their behalf.

Before engaging with the issue of the inalienability of sovereignty, Rousseau sets the scene for his argument by revisiting the grounds on which political societies are, according to him, formed in the first place:

> while the opposition of particular interests made the establishment of societies necessary, it is the agreement of those same interests which made it possible. What these different interests have in common is what forms the social bond, and if there were not some point on which all interests agree, no society could exist.
>
> (2.1.1)

In this passage, he tells us, then, that the people who unite together often have mutually antagonistic interests which threaten to lead them into conflict and mutual destruction but they also have interests in common and these shared interests make social co-operation possible. Implicit in what Rousseau says here is the thought that particular interest may be restrained for the sake of common interest. He will want to claim that there are possible terms of agreement between individuals that each person will have good and sufficient reason to accept. Those terms of association must safeguard our most fundamental interests, leaving each associate better off with respect to both security and freedom than he would be outside the association. The basic interest that each of us has in safeguarding our freedom underlies Rousseau's claim that sovereignty is essentially inalienable.

Rousseau has already made use of the term 'alienate' in Book 1, Chapter 4 where he defined it as meaning 'to give or to sell'. There, he had rejected the idea that a person could ever give up his freedom, his right to govern himself, in favour of someone else. To do this, he told us, would be to renounce one's essential human qualities and to deprive one's actions of all morality. Nevertheless, it very much looked as if, in entering the social pact, individuals had undertaken just such an act of alienation, though not in favour of some individual, but in favour of the community as a whole. So what is going on?

Rousseau writes that sovereignty 'since it is nothing but the exercise of the general will, can never be alienated' (2.1.2). This claim about the inalienability of sovereignty seems to derive from a more general thesis that *will* as such is inalienable, a thesis that Rousseau states explicity at 3.15.5: 'Sovereignty cannot be represented for the same reason that it cannot be alienated; it consists essentially in the general will, and the will does not admit of being represented'.

Here, Rousseau is implicitly responding to Hobbes's view that the will of a community might be vested in some particular person or persons. On this account, when people form themselves into a political community they authorise some person or body to bear or represent their collective personhood. Hobbes takes the word *authorise* literally. The members of the community are deemed to be the *authors* of the sovereign's actions. His actions are their actions, and for them to oppose some edict or command would be self-contradictory: they would be opposing their *own* pronouncements.

Rousseau wants to reject Hobbes's idea that the will of the sovereign can simply be imputed, jointly and severally, to the people. Rousseau would allow that a person can get another to act for him in a specific matter: I can ask a friend to post a letter for me. But the Hobbesian suggestion is that I can, in practice, cede to someone else the right to decide the basic direction of my life while continuing to be held responsible for each decision. Rousseau contends, by contrast, that in the legitimate social state persons will each, *in fact*, continue to be governed by a will that is *theirs*. Each person – *as a citizen* – has a general will which he exercises collectively. At 2.1.3 he wants to reject the notion that this general will could be exercised on behalf of the citizens by someone else or by some subset of the population and still *count* as their will.

Rousseau follows this discussion of the inalienability of sovereignty with a chapter claiming that sovereignty is also *indivisible*.

This doctrine has often been read as a rejection, by Rousseau, of the doctrine of the separation of powers. But this was *not* his intent. Rather, he wants to reinforce his rejection of the notion that sovereignty essentially consists in something other than the exercise of the general will by the people as a whole. A rival conception of sovereignty to Rousseau's own identifies it with the possession of a list of specific powers: 'Force and will, . . . legislative and executive power, . . . rights of taxation, justice and war . . . domestic administration and the power to conduct foreign affairs' (2.2.2).

But for Rousseau no such list of powers can capture the essence of sovereignty. These are all just applications of sovereignty rather than the thing itself. He thinks that to give such a list is rather like answering a request for a definition of voluntary action by providing a series of examples of actions that a person might freely perform.

These two chapters have left Rousseau with an awkward problem. He has rejected the idea that someone else might represent the sovereign. The sovereign – the people as a whole – must take its own decisions and decisions taken by others cannot be attributed to it. But he also wants to argue that *individuals* continue to govern themselves in the civil state, so he must believe that decisions taken by the collective can be attributed to the individuals who make it up. We shall see whether he can make good on this ambitious claim.

THE GENERAL WILL AND THE 'WILL OF ALL' (2.3.1–2)

The picture that Rousseau has given us so far is of a self-governing community and the impression we have probably gained of the general will, is that it consists in the collective decision of the people. The reader who has been proceeding on this understanding will encounter Book 2 Chapter 3 as a shock. This chapter, entitled 'Whether the General Will Can Err' begins by declaring that:

> From the preceding it follows that the general will is always upright and always tends to the public utility: but it does not follow from it that the people's deliberations are always equally upright. One always wants one's good, but one does not always see it: one can never

corrupt the people, but one can often cause it to be mistaken, and only when it is, does it appear to want what is bad.

(2.3.1)

It is actually anything but clear *why* the uprightness of the general will must follow from what has gone before. Perhaps Rousseau thinks that insofar as citizens constitute a collective body and identify with their role as members of that body they will desire to pursue its good (their common good). The important feature of this passage though, is that Rousseau is, here, making a sharp distinction between the general will on the one hand, and the decision of the people on the other. The general will, possessed by all of, and each of, the citizens, always wills the common good. But if the people are misled as to matters of fact or reasoning they may misidentify what conduces to their good.

Rousseau's thought here needs a little reconstruction. He appears to believe that it is a necessary truth, for any willing being, that it wills its own good. But there is a crucial distinction to be drawn between willing one's good and wanting what is good for one. If I am misinformed, or I reason badly, I will end up wanting things that are not, actually, congenial to the good that I will. In pursuit of my own good I may act contrary to my own best interests. Here, he is invoking, in effect, a Socratic distinction between doing what a person wants and thus doing what they will.[2] For Socrates, human beings always will the good (an even stronger claim than that they always will *their* good). So, for example, in the *Protagoras* Socrates observes:

> I am pretty sure that none of the wise men thinks that any human being willingly makes a mistake or willingly does anything wrong or bad. They know very well that anyone who does anything wrong or bad does so involuntarily.[3]

And in the *Gorgias*, Socrates argues that all action aims at the good of the person who acts but that, through defects of knowledge, people often pursue aims that are not actually beneficial to them. On Socrates' account, even those who appear to have absolute power are rendered powerless by lack of intelligence: 'I say . . . that both orators and tyrants have the least power in their cities . . . For they do just about nothing they want to, though they certainly do whatever they see most fit to do'.[4]

The proposition that people never knowingly pursue a goal that they know to be bad for them, is far from being obviously true,[5] but it is clear from his remarks here and from his statement at 2.1.2 that 'no will can consent to anything contrary to the good of the being that wills' that Rousseau endorses such a picture of motivation. His suggestion, on this reading, is that the citizens, assembled as an artificial body – a 'being of reason' – are necessarily led to seek their own good, but that cognitive defects and epistemic obstacles often cause them to mistake where that good lies. But this transition from a questionable psychological thesis about individuals to a claim about the nature of an artificial collective body composed of many natural persons is hardly without difficulties.

The first obvious problem is that such 'willing' as the artificial being does, depends directly on the willing of the natural persons who make it up. Rousseau needs to give us reason to believe that those persons are normally going to pursue their good in the assembly in a manner that is consistent with the general will. Why would they not simply pursue their *particular* interests at the expense of the common good? The only answer consistent with the Socratic thesis is to say that if citizens were properly informed about their own good, they would will, as an essential component and prerequisite of that good, the common good. An argument for that claim would depend on citizens satisfying their most fundamental interests only on condition that they associate together (a thought that Rousseau has already articulated at 1.6.1). As we have seen, Rousseau does indeed subscribe to such an argument. But even if the citizens perceive that their individual good is necessarily tied up with the common good, Rousseau will still need to make the step from individuals seeking that good to the collective successfully doing so.

Rousseau addresses the question of the connection between individual and collective good and between individual willing and collective decision in successive paragraphs. At 2.3.2 he writes one of the most obscure and argued-over passages of the entire *Social Contract*:

> There is often a considerable difference between the will of all and the general interest: the latter looks only to the common interest, the former looks to private interest and is nothing more than a sum of particular wills; but if, from those same wills, one takes away the pluses and the minuses which cancel each other out, what is left as the sum of the differences is the general will.

Rousseau's reference to the 'pluses and minuses' is an attempt to make an analogy between the process of aggregating different wills to arrive at the general will and the operation of integration in infinitesimal calculus. As such, it is likely to obscure as much as it is to enlighten. But his underlying thought seems to be that private or particular interest of individuals and their common interest stand in a definite relationship to one another and that the general will could, in principle, be derived from the collected particular wills of individuals by an operation that somehow smoothed out, as it were, the differences between them. The 'raw' private wills, added together, here constitute the 'will of all'; the general will is derived from those same wills, subject to some processing.

Rousseau tries to clarify his distinction between the will of all and the general will with a footnote reference to the Marquis d'Argenson where the Marquis states: 'the agreement between all interests is framed by opposition to each one's interest.'[6] Rousseau's thought here is that it is in each person's interest that the pursuit of self-interest by others be restrained. This suggests that the common interest will always have as part of its content, rules which it would be advantageous to each for all to comply with.[7] That might give the impression that the state governed by the general will might be quite minimal in character, involving the protection and enforcement of a sparse set of individual rights. But the opposition between interests may also support conventions governing the distribution of property. So, for example, we might imagine some good which it is in each person's interest to have as much of as possible. Each person then has a private interest in getting as much of that good as he can. But in a free-for-all each risks getting nothing, or worse. So each person has an interest in opposing the claims of any particular person on the good in question in favour of arguing for some principle of fair division. In the absence of any complicating factors the salient principle is likely to be one of *equality*. Moreover, this principle is likely to be one which each individual senses as directly relevant to his own interests and will consequently be moved to advance according to the general will which is *his*. Now this is a highly simplified example, and in other cases the rule that corresponds to the common interest will be less easy to determine. The suggestion, though, is that the general will is not arrived at by simply assembling the maximal demands of individuals (the will of all) but, rather, through a rational consideration of how those interests may be furthered, given a similar pursuit of interest by others.

VOTING AND THE PROBLEM OF FACTION (2.3.3–4)

Rousseau next addresses the problem of aggregating the interests of the many and various citizens together: 'If when an adequately informed people deliberates, the Citizens had no communication among themselves, the general will would always result from the large number of small differences, and the deliberation would always be good' (2.3.3).

Rousseau goes on to say that where citizens do not make up their minds independently of one another but are, rather, grouped into stable coalitions and factions, the danger is that a majority will be secured in the assembly that does not reflect the common interest but rather the will of one of these subgroups. Recall our example of dividing some good among persons. If citizens are confronted with a choice between a free-for-all and fair division, they have good reason to choose the latter. But suppose they could form a coalition to divide the good equally among a subset of the population while leaving a minority with little or nothing. Clearly, if citizens' sole interest is to do as well for themselves privately as they can, they will be tempted to form such a self-serving coalition. But if they succeed in doing so, it will no longer be the general will of the community as a whole that prevails but, rather, a will that is general in relation to their faction, but particular in relation to society as a whole. Rousseau wants to avoid such coalition-formation against the common interest and so argues that citizens should cast their votes separately with 'no communication' among themselves and that factions in the assembly of citizens should be forbidden, but that, failing this, the number of such 'partial societies' should be multiplied so that no faction can dominate.

Note that it is far from clear what, exactly, Rousseau means when he says that citizens should have 'no communication' (2.3.3). Though it is natural to read this as saying that citizens should not *talk* to one another, this goes beyond what Rousseau needs and seems completely incompatible with any realistic view of what would happen in any society. A more plausible suggestion would be just that citizens cast their votes independently of one another via some mechanism like the secret ballot so that it would be impossible for any coalition to enforce discipline.[8]

Rousseau's concern with the distorting influence of faction on the emergence of the general will from the deliberations of the assembly surfaces again and again in the *Social Contract*. He returns to this problem at the beginning of Book 4. At 4.1.6 he writes of the citizen in a corrupt state at the edge of ruin:

> . . . instead of saying with his vote, *it is advantageous to the State*, he says, *it is advantageous to this man or to this party that this or that opinion pass*. Thus the law of public order in assemblies consists not so much of upholding the general will in them, as in seeing to it that the general will is always consulted and that it always replies.

And in the immediately following chapter he again warns against the influence of factions:

> The more concord reigns in assemblies, that is to say the closer opinions come to unanimity, the more the general will also predominates; whereas long debates, dissensions, disturbances, signal the ascendancy of particular interests and the decline of the State.
>
> (4.2.1, see also 4.2.9–10)

Rousseau's preferred method for preventing the emergence of factions is to ensure the simplicity, equality and transparency of the state. Ideally, 'several men united consider themselves a single body' (4.1.1), and the people most likely to do this are 'troops of peasants ... seen attending to the affairs of State under an oak tree and always acting wisely'. Rustic simplicity, combined with a small size for the state and a rough equality of fortune, surfaces repeatedly in Rousseau's work, from the *Dedicace* to the *Discourse on Inequality* through to the *Social Contract*. And we have seen the importance that he attaches to property distribution at 1.9.8n.

It is worth comparing Rousseau's concern with faction to the response to the same problem given by another eighteenth-century political thinker, James Madison. Madison outlines the problem:

> By a faction I understand a number of citizens, whether amounting to a majority or a minority of the whole, who are united and actuated by some common impulse of passion, or of interest, adverse to the rights of other citizens, or to the permanent and aggregate interests of the community.[9]

Madison argues that we can either remove the causes of faction or we can seek to mitigate its effects. There are two ways in which the causes of faction can be disposed of: either citizens can be deprived of liberty, or we can seek to give 'to every citizen the same opinions, the same passions, and the same interests'. Madison opposes both of these methods; Rousseau toys with each of them. At 2.3.4, where he insists on the importance of there being 'no partial society in the State' it is freedom of association that he comes close to rejecting, and he seems to hold back less on grounds of principle than of practicality. And in his vaunting of the example of the 'troops of peasants' as well as in some of the more extreme passages of *Emile* on 'denaturing', he appears to advocate a homogeneity of opinion and the suppression of any individualism. Yet these passages are balanced by others, such as 2.4.2 where he insists on the 'natural independence' of the 'private persons' who make up the sovereign, and by the final full chapter of the *Social Contract*, on civil religion, where he accepts the inevitability of a diversity of opinion.

Here is not the place to reflect at any length about the comparative merits of Rousseau's small homogeneous state and Madison's representative federal republic. Rousseau's recommendations have never been put into practice whereas Madison's have issued in a large and powerful state. To compare the ideal with the actual is always an unfair and distorting method. We cannot, therefore, test whether Rousseau's means of preventing the causes of faction would have been more effective than Madison's devices for mitigating its effects have been. It is, though, perhaps reasonable to wonder whether a small republic of virtue such as Rousseau proposed was really in keeping with his feasibility constraint – 'men as they are, laws as they can be'. Certainly, Hume doubted the relevance of the Spartan model – which Rousseau refers to at 2.3.4 – to the modern world, and many have agreed with him.[10]

A BRIEF NOTE ON CONDORCET'S JURY THEOREM

One way of reading Rousseau's account of the working of the assembly is to see it as concerned with addressing a question of fact. On this view, the question of what proposal answers to the general will has a correct answer, and the assembly is best understood as an epistemic device for getting at that answer. This view of the assembly and the general will get some support from other passages in the *Social Contract* (e.g. 4.2.8). Following this line of thought, some commentators and interpreters have seen in the two final paragraphs of 2.3 an anticipation of Condorcet's jury theorem, although the evidence of any direct connection between the two men is weak.[11] Condorcet's ideas do offer some support, however, to Rousseau's claim that if properly informed citizens were to deliberate, and to decide separately, then the general will would emerge from a vote of the assembly. While there is a chance that each citizen, though well intentioned, will be mistaken about whether a proposal accords with the general will, Condorcet shows that providing only that each citizen has a better than 50:50 chance of being right, then as the number of citizens increases, the probability of the majority being right gets closer and closer to 1.[12] The condition that each person casts their votes independently of each other person is crucial here. If the way I vote depends causally on the way you vote then the number of genuinely independent voices diminishes to that same extent: at the limit case, if all follow one leader then the competence of the group will be no higher than the competence of that one person. Hence, another difficulty with the emergence of factions in the assembly is that instead of being able to draw on the competence of the citizens as a whole, only the ability of those in command of parties will be reflected.

THE LIMITS OF SOVEREIGN POWER AND THE NATURE OF THE LAW (2.4, 2.6)

In Chapters 4 to 6 of Book 2, Rousseau further explores the nature of sovereignty, making good on his promise in the very first paragraph of the book to 'combine what right permits with what interest prescribes'. His contention is that, when the nature of the sovereign is understood properly, the standard liberal concerns about the power of the state and the liberty of the individual disappear: sovereign power is, in its essence, self-limiting. We may not, in the end, be fully persuaded by Rousseau's attempt to finesse the traditional liberal concern. Nevertheless, an examination of his arguments should at least further clarify his understanding of the concepts of sovereignty and the general will.

The sovereign, Rousseau tells us, is an artificial body (a 'moral person' 2.4.1) composed of natural individuals who have associated together to preserve their lives. As such, the sovereign answers to their most basic interest in survival. The renunciation of the right to pursue one's ends without regard to the good of others that individuals make with the social pact cannot, rationally, entail a submission to the will of some other particular individual. As we have seen that would be contrary to one's nature and no guarantee of survival at all. Rather, individuals submit not to the will of any other person but subject themselves to a set of general conditions or conventions that they themselves have willed. The form these conventions take, from the perspective of each citizen, is that they place the same limits on the freedom of others that persons are willing to accept for themselves. There is thus a mutuality and a reciprocity about sovereign acts: I impose no condition on you that I am not also prepared to accept for myself.

There is though, no pre-established restriction in principle, to what the citizens may legislate on. In this respect, Rousseau adopts a Hobbesian view of sovereignty, but whereas for Hobbes, someone acting with our 'authority' can have absolute power, for Rousseau, the people collectively do so. The reader who considers the prospect of unlimited sovereignty with alarm, may encounter Rousseau's discussion at 2.4.2 with surprise and relief. Having just told us that the social pact gives the body politic absolute power over its members and that sovereignty is the exercise of this power by the general will, Rousseau immediately seeks to make a distinction between the public person and the private persons who compose it and whose 'life and freedom are naturally independent of it'. He then invites us to distinguish, first between the rights of the sovereign and those of the citizen and between the duties the citizens have as subjects and the 'natural right' that they continue to enjoy as men. Adding apparent confusion on apparent confusion, he seems to contradict what he said at 1.6.6 about the total alienation of each person's rights to the community by telling us that 'each man alienates by the social pact only that portion of his power, his goods, his freedom, which it is important for the community to be able to use', but then seems to immediately take away this concession by leaving the judgement of what is important entirely in the hands of the sovereign![13]

So is there *really* a contradiction here? Despite appearances, Rousseau is not trying to pick out some reserved private sphere where the sovereign has no right to intrude: there are indeed no rights which the individual has held back at the moment of the social pact. Rather, Rousseau wants to tell us that sovereignty – properly constituted – poses no threat to (and indeed is essential to) individual autonomy. His thought is that citizens, when willing the general will, are willing general obligations and rules that apply to each alike. It is the generality of these rules, and the fact that they are willed by all and apply to all that is the real limit on tyrannical power. As Rousseau puts it: 'the Sovereign power . . . does not and cannot exceed the limits of the general conventions' (2.4.9).

'UNIVERSALITY OF THE WILL AND OF THE OBJECT'

In a series of passages in Chapters 4 and 6, Rousseau expands on the working of the general will and on his belief that the laws will have an equitable character. The most extended of these passages is at 2.4.5:

> The commitments which bind us to the social body are obligatory only because they are mutual, and their nature is such that in fulfilling them one cannot work for others without also working for oneself. Why is the general will always upright, and why do all consistently will each one's happiness, if not because there is no one who does not appropriate the word *each* to himself, and think of himself as he votes for all? Which proves that the equality of right and the notion of justice which it produces follows from each one's preference for himself and hence from the nature of man; that the general will, to be truly such, must be so in its object as well as its essence, that it must issue from all in order to apply to all, and that it loses its natural rectitude when it tends towards some individual and determinate object; for then, judging what is foreign to us, we have no true principle of equity to guide us.
>
> (2.4.5, see also 2.4.7 and 2.6.8)

However much the institutions of a just society reshape human beings, it is clear from this passage that such denaturing has definite limits. 'Men as they are' always retain a sense of self and of self-interest that is distinct from society as a whole. They are never wholly engulfed by their common identity as citizens but always retain a private identity as men.

How are we to understand Rousseau's requirement that the general will must come from all and apply to all? The requirement that acts of the sovereign apply to all is a requirement that no one should be outside the law. There are to be no laws which apply to some people or some groups of people and not to others. That is not to say that there may not be laws which impact on some people more than others, or which affect some people not at all. A law which prescribes a universal rule of the road will affect motorists far more than it will those who do not drive. Certainly, the law must not name individuals – that would be a clear loss of generality – but it would also be unacceptable for the law to use definite descriptions to single out one group for special treatment. In practice, it is not always easy to say in advance about a law whether its generality is merely formal or genuinely substantive. But it is at least possible to give examples of laws that substantively pass or fail the condition of applying to all. So, for example, a law requiring all keepers of motor vehicles to ensure that their tyres are in a safe condition does substantively meet the condition of applying to all, whereas a law stating that everyone with blue eyes or brown skin should pay a special tax does not.

The requirement that the law should come from all is a requirement that each person should have a good reason to accept the law. We already have some idea of what these good reasons shareable by all might consist in. Associates continue to possess interests and desires which issue from their nature as separate natural human beings. Those human beings have chosen to associate together in order to escape the defects of the state of nature, but they retain a keen sense of individual interest. They will, therefore, have good reason to agree to laws that ensure their peace, freedom and security. This will mean that they will have reason to assent to laws which permit to each of them such freedom as is compatible with a like freedom for all. Given the insecurity and practical unfreedom associated with the immediately pre-political condition, citizens will also have reason to assent to laws which tend to the preservation and well-functioning of their association. Accordingly, laws which regulate holdings of property to ensure a rough equality of fortune and measures to promote social harmony and solidarity – such as the civil religion – should, according to Rousseau, also find favour with each associate.

Rousseau's discussion in these chapters is noteworthy as an anticipation of the work of later social contract theorists (such as John Rawls's original position). He is attempting to devise a procedure which will harness the natural self-love (*amour de soi*) that he believes necessarily motivates people and redirect that passion in a way that necessarily results in an equitable outcome. Rousseau's individuals are constrained by the form that law must take if it is to count as law (and also by such further conditions as the need to decide independently of one another), but, unlike Rawls's contractors, they decide on the laws in full knowledge of their identities, their physical and intellectual strengths and weaknesses, their views about morality, of what is valuable in life, and so forth. Of course, this has to be so, since unlike Rawls, Rousseau is designing a procedure for real (rather than hypothetical) deliberation and decision. But, if conditions similar to those Rawlsian ones do not form a part of Rousseau's construction, there is clearly a problem. The procedure that Rousseau outlines may enhance the possibility that the outcome of sovereign deliberation will be equitable, but it cannot *guarantee* such a result.

If the merely formal condition that the law be general in its object cannot assure an outcome that is just, what can? The short answer is: nothing. In political life there can be no absolute certainties. But Rousseau has much to say about further conditions that must obtain. When he says that the general will must 'issue from all in order to apply to all' (2.4.6), he is not just reiterating a formal constraint, but is also, implicitly, reiterating the concern with factional division that he had expressed at 2.3.3–4. And if the likely source of faction is inequality in wealth and income, we see how essential it is to the good functioning of the state that a rough material equality is maintained among its members. If rough material equality does not obtain then it will be possible for something to take the *form* of the general will, being a declaration which comes from the collective body and applies to all equally, but not to have its substance (because of the very different impact that the would-be expression of the general will has on different citizens). For Rousseau's attempt to finesse the problem of public power and individual liberty through a consideration of the essential nature of sovereignty, it has to be the case that when citizens deliberate 'there is no one who does not appropriate the word *each* to himself, and think of himself as he votes for all'. Not only must citizens think of themselves, it must also be the case that when they do so they are thereby pursuing interests that they share in common with others. In a simple and homogeneous society this will be the case, but in a deeply divided one even the contemplation of abstract rules applying to all will not result in the common interest since each person will look to how such rules impact on members of their group rather than on themselves as citizens.

There are further obstacles to the successful emergence of the general will that Rousseau does not sufficiently consider. He is very concerned that citizens might divide on class lines, but other sources of social division seem to pass him by. This is a little surprising since, in the final full chapter of the *Social Contract*, the chapter on 'civil religion', he presupposes the existence of confessional differences among the citizens. Even though Rousseau is largely silent about the details of this issue, we should assume that when the lawgiver sets about his work of forging a people, the task of ensuring the primacy of their patriotic identity as citizens over other, particular, attachments, will be one of his priorities.

THE DEATH PENALTY (2.5)

Rousseau completes his discussion of the limits of sovereign power with a discussion of cases where the state takes the life of its citizens. There seem to be two problems here, both of which arise from the contractual basis of the state. The first is to explain how the state can have the right to kill people when they do not have the natural right to kill themselves. If the rights of the state derive from the rights of individuals, how can the state have a right that the individual never had? The second is how the state can have the right to kill its subjects given that their motive for entering the political order is (partly) the preservation of their lives.

Rousseau's answer is to tell us that willing the end of personal security through the state also implies willing the means, and that in order for the state to subsist it is sometimes necessary for people to risk their lives. Since each person is willing as a condition of their own security that others risk their lives for him, Rousseau claims that reciprocity requires that he be willing to risk his life for them. He then claims that a parallel argument applies in the case of the death penalty which the citizen consents to as a means of preserving their own life and not with the aim of losing it.

Both cases are presented as rational gambles that may turn out badly. He then goes on to present a second argument (2.5.4) whereby criminals may be considered as having placed themselves outside the state or even at war with it so that they may be killed by the right of war. This is in sharp contradiction to the argument he puts at 1.4.9 whereby war is, by its very nature, a relationship between states.

One difficulty with Rousseau's argument here is its consistency with the immediately preceding section 'Of the Limits of the Sovereign Power'. There Rousseau had insisted that the sovereign people could not even will to put in place any 'shackles that are useless to the community' (2.4.4). A well-ordered state will presumably be one whose very existence is not threatened by criminal violence. Not only should there be fewer criminals in a state where the social spirit is strong, it should be possible to restrain those that remain by less severe measures than execution. This consideration was invoked when the French revolutionaries debated the measure, and both opponents of, and enthusiasts for, the death penalty sought to rely on Rousseau in their arguments.[14]

THE LAW (FURTHER ASPECTS) (2.6)

Rousseau's chapter on the nature of law seems rather curious to the reader since he appears to be going over ground which has already been covered. So, for example, when Rousseau tells us that the 'object of the laws is always general' (2.6.6) he is repeating what he told us about the characteristics of the general will in 2.4. One possible explanation for this is that the discussion has taken a turn in the direction of greater concreteness in anticipation of the chapters to come on the legislator (2.7) and the discussion of government in Book 3. This reading is supported by the way in which Rousseau begins by telling us that although the social pact has brought the political community into existence (so it already has a general will) it now has to take the actions necessary in order to subsist.

In a fascinating paragraph (2.6.2) Rousseau explains his view of the relationship between divine law and human law, and, in the process, tacitly distances himself from Montesquieu. In *The Spirit of the Laws* Montesquieu had advanced an account of human law as being continuous with divine law:

> Laws, in their most general signification, are the necessary relations arising from the nature of things. In this sense all beings have their laws: the Deity His laws, the material world its laws, the intelligences superior to man their laws, the beasts their laws, man his laws . . . There is, then, a prime reason; and laws are the relations subsisting between it and different beings, and the relations of these to one another.[15]

Rousseau is far from being simply dismissive of the idea of law as expressing a cosmic well-orderedness. Indeed, in both the *Profession of Faith of the Savoyard Vicar* and in the *Lettres Morales* he ascribes to the faculty of conscience an innate sensitivity to that very feature of the world. But the *Social Contract* is directed to the human situation where that natural harmony has been irretrievably lost. Given 'men as they are' we must use artifice in the form of positive institutions to secure our good. As he made clear in 'The General Society of the Human Race', the person who abides by laws of abstract morality without a guarantee that others will also abide by them simply opens himself to exploitation by others: 'the laws of justice are vain among men for want of natural sanctions' (2.6.2). The civil state ends – or at least diminishes – the uncertainty that the good face and will give them an assurance of one another's conduct as well as establishing settled conventions that they can all rely upon concerning things such as property. It achieves this not by projecting a natural order onto human society, but by getting the flawed human beings who associate together to consider which institutions would best advance their interests.

Rousseau now repeats and elaborates his claim that there can be no general will about a particular object. He tells us that a particular object is either inside or outside the state. Since the general will must come from all and apply to all and manifestly does not come from whatever is outside the state, the will of the members of the state is not general in relation to that object. Where the object is within the state we find the state divided, effectively, into two factions: those possessing some particular interest in common and the rest, with there being no general will in relation to either. The law is always general in its form and addresses the people's actions in the abstract: it does not name individuals. This does not mean that laws cannot differentially affect citizens. Rousseau puts forward a number of examples of ways in which the law can create privileges or positions, and presumably the possessors of those privileges or offices benefit from them. But the justification for voting on such measures would have to be that they are in the common interest. It would be wrong for someone to favour the establishment of some particular office because of their estimation of their chance of obtaining it.

With the final paragraph of 2.6, Rousseau returns to the difficult question of how to ensure that the people promulgate laws that are, in fact, in their common interest. It is essential that the people and the people alone is the author of the laws. This is necessary if the condition that citizens obey only themselves is to be met. But the putative authors of the laws may be cognitively ill-equipped for their task. They may lack the necessary foresight. Rousseau repeats the claim that the people always wills the good. That is to say that the people always want whatever it is that is in their best common interest, but although they seek the good for themselves they may be mistaken as to where it lies and so may fail to pass the laws they should.

MORE ON THE GENERAL WILL (4.1–2)

The picture we obtain of the sovereign assembly and the general will from the first part of Book 2 needs to be supplemented by remarks that Rousseau makes elsewhere, most notably in the first two chapters of Book 4. There, he operates with an explicit contrast between a well-ordered and a degenerate state. In states composed of simple unsophisticated men, who share common mores and enjoy a rough equality of fortune, political discussion is straightforward and there is no difficulty in perceiving where the common interest lies. Matters are quite otherwise in a complex and unequal society composed of sophisticates where opinion rules. There:

when particular interests begin to make themselves felt and small societies to influence the larger society, the common interest diminishes and meets with opposition, votes are no longer unanimous, the general will is no longer the will of all, contradictions and disagreements arise, and the best opinion no longer carries the day unchallenged.

(4.1.4)

Here again, Rousseau emphasises the distorting influence that small societies can bring to bear so that the vote of the citizens fails to express the general will. Moreover, in an atmosphere of faction and machination, the attitude of citizens to voting also changes, everyone is 'prompted by secret motives'(4.1.5). Rousseau's concern here may seem a little odd. After all, when he had earlier discussed the motivation of citizens in voting, he had advanced as one of the reasons for the *uprightness* of the general will that 'there is no-one who does not appropriate the word *each* to himself, and think of himself as he votes for all' (2.4.5). The difference between the two instances is that in the latter, the citizen is constrained to think of himself as an undifferentiated member of the polity and thus to seek his own good through the good of the society as a whole. But in the former, he focuses on the possible advantage accruing to himself as a member of a faction or a supporter of this or that demagogue and asks himself whether 'it is advantageous to this man or this party that this or that opinion pass' (4.1.6). In each case he seeks his own advantage in accordance with 'each one's preference for himself and hence from the nature of man', but when he votes as citizen he associates that advantage with the advantage of all through impartial law, whereas when he votes as a faction member he connects his well-being with that of a sub-group.

Rousseau has claimed that, in a society governed according to the general will, no individual is subordinate to a will that is not his own. This freedom-preserving requirement is perhaps the most important single difference between Hobbes and Rousseau. It is, therefore, surprising when we encounter Rousseau's explicit attempt to address the compatibility of individual autonomy with majority rule. At 4.2.6 Rousseau explains that the social pact itself requires unanimity, but in the succeeding paragraph he explains that ordinary laws do not:

> ... the vote of the majority always obligates all the rest; this is a consequence of the contract itself. Yet the question is raised how a man can be both free and forced to conform to laws which are not his own. How are the opponents both free and subject to laws to which they have not consented?

Rousseau has answered the question of how the associated can be free but subject to laws twice already. At 1.7.8 in the 'forced to be free' passage he had explained that since laws provide a guarantee against personal dependence everyone has good reason to submit to them. At 2.6.8 he had described the laws as 'merely records of our wills', and since one can hardly be said to be unfree in conforming to one's own will, the issue seemed easily closed. But here he addresses the question of being subject to laws that one has voted against. How can this count as an instance of being subject to one's own will? Rousseau's response seems to be that even in this case they will the general will but are mistaken as to its content:

> When a law is proposed in the People's assembly, what they are being asked is not exactly whether they approve the proposal or reject it, but whether it does or does not conform to the general will which is theirs; everyone states his opinion about this by casting his ballot, and the tally of the votes yields the declaration of the general will. Therefore, when the opinion contrary to my own prevails, it proves nothing more than that I made a mistake and that what I took to be the general will was not. If my particular opinion had prevailed, I would have done something other than what I had willed, and it is then that I would not have been free.
>
> (4.2.8)

There is a slight infelicity in Rousseau's expression here since, of course, *if* my particular opinion *had* prevailed in the assembly, this would have shown it to be in accordance with the general will! One possible way of reading Rousseau's thought here would refer back to the Socratic claim that citizens always will their good even when they misperceive where it lies. On this view, since the sovereign assembly is a normally reliable device for finding out where that common good lies, the effect of submitting to laws I did not vote for is to secure what I will, even though I was mistaken about what that willing required. The more indirect story is that given that I have decided that my best interests are served by being in political society – by being a citizen rather than not – I have an interest in securing and agreeing upon fair general principles by which all should regulate their conduct. The procedures of the assembly are such as to ensure the emergence of such principles and I will what emerges from the procedure even when my antecedent supposition about what would emerge was flawed.

Many have thought that Rousseau's suggestion here is outlandish, but we can see that it is not necessarily so by considering a parallel case. Suppose a group of friends wants to go out together. They may have different ideas about what would be best, but each expresses an opinion in favour of some activity or other, and a decision is taken. I might have wanted to go bowling, but I did not want to go bowling alone, and so I will that the most popular particular activity (which turns out, against my antecendent desire and expectation, to be a Chinese meal) be the one in which we engage.

My core interest is in a continuing relationship with my fellow citizens on fair terms and since that is what I most deeply want, I get what I want when the conditions for maintaining that relationship are secured even when I had different views about how that might be brought about.

Rousseau adds an intriguing qualification to his claim that what emerges from the procedures of the assembly is in accordance with the general will:

> This presupposes, it is true, that all the characteristics of the general will are still in the majority: once they no longer are, then regardless of which side one takes there is no longer any freedom.
>
> (4.2.9)

This somewhat cryptic remark is an allusion to the problem of faction that he had earlier discussed at 2.3.3–4 and at 4.1.6. If society is divided and citizens vote, not in pursuit of an interest that they share with everyone but, rather, in pursuit of a sectional interest, then the assembly ceases to be a reliable mechanism for discerning where the common interest lies and what emerges from the deliberations and voting of the assembly no longer reflects the general will.

So, although Rousseau believes that it is a necessary condition of legitimate authority that the citizens promulgate the laws according to their common interests, and that procedures can be designed so that decisions tend reliably to track that common interest, there can be no guarantee of political success: 'If Sparta and Rome perished, what state can hope to last forever?' (3.11.1).

SYNOPTIC REMARKS ON THE GENERAL WILL

At the outset of this chapter, I distinguished between the idea of the general will as the collective decision, and the idea of the general will as the standard to which that decision should conform. We have also noticed that the general will seems to be not only a property of the people as a whole, but also of each one of the several individuals who make it up. Rousseau has suggested that both individuals and the people as a whole can be mistaken about the content of the general will. He has told us that even when no one is moved to pursue the general will, it somehow persists, as pure as ever. He has defined sovereignty as the direction of the state according to the general will. He also tells us that sovereignty resides in the people as a whole and that no one else – no group or individual – can exercise sovereignty in their name. He tells us that when individuals obey the general will, they obey themselves.

It is a formidable task to reconcile these competing statements and what follows is just one suggestion for how this might be done. The first thing to note is that Rousseau tells us that individuals have an interest in getting out of a pre-political state where they inevitably thwart the pursuit of one another's aims and, indeed, endanger one another's very survival. That being so, they have a very concrete common interest in establishing and maintaining terms of co-operation among themselves: rules to regulate their common conduct. Such terms of co-operation cannot simply be intuited by individuals using their private reason and voluntarily obeyed: there is too much scope for disagreement, no reliable mechanism of enforcement and the capacity for such abstract generalisation is, anyway, the fruit of participation in legal and political institutions and so cannot substitute for them. Nor is the imposition of a set of rules by someone else an option for Rousseau. There is no good reason to suppose that such an imposition would genuinely promote the common interest and, in fact, grounds for thinking that such a person or persons would inevitably favour themselves.

Accordingly, the pursuit and identification of the common interest which we each have a share in can only be the task of the group, the people, as a whole. It is only by deliberating together that we can establish what is really in our common interest. But there is a difficulty: it is a matter of fact whether or not any given proposal is genuinely in our common interest, but any human procedures to discover whether or not this is so are *fallible*. Hence, there can be no absolute guarantee that our common deliberations will issue in laws and regulations that authentically promote the common interest.

In particular, there is a danger that the particular interests – whose fatal opposition to one another necessitated the formation of the state in the first place – will get promoted, rather than the interests in mutual restraint of one another's conduct that individuals share. Rousseau thinks that this undesirable outcome will normally be avoided if the people are properly and adequately informed and by the fact that the law consists of general regulations that apply to all citizens impartially, just so long as citizens do not become grouped into factions, particularly factions based on divisions between rich and poor. If such factions do emerge, it is likely that the law will then reflect the common interest of a sub-group rather than that of the citizens as a whole. Accordingly, practical measures are needed to guard against the formation of coalitions.

Given that Rousseau accepts that the process of collective deliberation can result in decisions that fail to accord with the general will – and indeed tells us that when the state is at the edge of ruin and public discourse is entirely subverted by private machinations the general will persists, as pure as ever – it is tempting to plump for an account of the general will that divorces it from the empirical willing of citizens. This way of reading Rousseau, identifying the general will with the true collective interest, regardless of what citizens happen think about the matter, is found in much post-Rousseauian writing, especially the German idealist current that runs through Kant and Hegel to Hegelian Marxists such as Gyorgy Lukacs. But such an account sits ill with Rousseau's characterisation of the nature of sovereignty. So, for example, he says in the *Geneva Manuscript* that 'There is therefore in the State a common force which sustains it, a general will which directs this force and it is the application of the one to the other which constitutes sovereignty'.[16] In this passage the directing general will plainly involves the deliberation and decision of the citizens.

We can bridge the gap somewhat if we remember Rousseau's view that so long as the people are properly informed, decide independently, and avoid faction, popular deliberation is *normally* a reliable mechanism for securing the common interest. The deliberating people are normally authoritative about the common interest and consequently their deliberations are usually to be taken as expressions of the general will. But what of the allegedly asymptomatic persistence of the general will when the state is factionally divided? Here, it seems natural to make a distinction between the two conditions of the general will: the general will accompanied by a specific content, and a more indeterminate condition of the general will. When Rousseau tells us that citizens, individually and collectively, always will the general will, he means that they always will whatever is in the common interest. But it is possible to will whatever is in the common interest without being clear and, indeed, while being mistaken, about where that common interest lies. In order to establish *that* we need actual deliberation by citizens who bring their concrete interests to the forum.

In the case where collective deliberation misfires, and a decision is reached that is not in accordance with the general will, we may be tempted to say that the general will has some specific content which the citizens have failed to will and we might identify this content with what they would have willed had their deliberation accorded with some ideal procedural model.[17] But there is no requirement to approach matters in this way. An analogy with individual action and decision may help here. There are many different ways in which a person can be irrational. So, when King George III of England greeted an oak tree in the belief that he was hailing the King of Prussia he was being irrational in one way, whereas people who prefer to be in the country when they are in the city but in the city when they are in the country are irrational in another. We can convict such persons of irrationality without having a complete positive account of how they should have acted. Normally, we take (adult) persons to be authoritative about what is in their best interests. But we are aware of many cases where people act contrary to those best interests and we can often give an account of how and why they do so. In similar fashion, then, we take the people as a whole to be normally authoritative about the content of their common interest, while accepting that sometimes their decision will go wrong. In the cases where it does plainly go wrong, we can say that they have failed to decide according to their general will, without committing ourselves to the general will mandating some other specific decision. The approach I am advocating, then, says that, so long as the assembly is properly constituted and its procedures are followed against a suitable background of cultural and economic similarity of life, then we must take the decision of the people to be indicative of the general will. Where those conditions fail, for whatever reason, the general will may persist as an intention of each citizen, but it is an intention that lacks expression or, indeed, determinate content.

It is appropriate to end our discussion of the general will with an indication of its incompleteness so far. Rousseau may sometimes have given the impression that the general will can emerge by a consideration of each citizen's rational self-interest where that self-interest is suitably constrained by procedure (2.4.5). But though right reason in its pure form, guided by conscience, might conduce to the willing of the general will we are, after all, dealing with 'men as they are'. And men as they are are just as likely to put their capacity for reasoning in the service of their short-sighted passions as they are to be guided by reason as such. Rousseau is pessimistic that the consideration of rational self-interest would provide sufficient social solidarity to unite a political order:

> . . . the reasoning and philosophic spirit in general . . . causes attachment to life, makes souls effeminate and degraded, concentrates all the passions in the baseness of private interest, in the abjectness of the human *I*, and thus quietly saps the true foundations of every society. For what private interests have in common is so slight that it will never overcome what sets them in opposition.
>
> (E4: 312n/OC4: 632–3)

It may well be that prudence and rationality ought to lead us to co-operate together, guided by considerations of the common interest. But we are weak and we are passionate and Rousseau believes that we need to be bonded to our fellows by a genuine sense of moral unity. Providing this sense of moral cohesiveness is part of the task of the lawgiver – whom we shall encounter in the next chapter – and of the civil religion.

NOTES

1 Letter 2028 in CC, XII, p. 96.
2 See Dent, *Rousseau*, p. 247, n.6.
3 *Protagoras* 345e, from Plato, *Complete Works*.
4 *Gorgias* 466d, in ibid.
5 For a compelling fictional portrait of someone who knowingly abandons the good in favour of the worse, see Roth, *The Professor of Desire*.
6 Or, more accurately, the Marquis uses the words 'by an opposing reason' in his *Considerations on the Ancient and Present Government of France*. See the note at OC3: 1456.
7 We can anticipate, then, that most of the laws of nature outlined by Hobbes or Locke would be willed by the general will.

8 Not that Rousseau is unconcerned about what happens when citizens do discuss. In particular, he is worried about the possible influence of demagogues. See, for example, the passages in the *Discourse on Political Economy* where he discusses the problem of 'eloquence' (G2: 8/OC3: 246).

9 Madison and Hamilton, *The Federalist Papers* X, p. 123.

10 See Hume's essay 'Of Commerce'.

11 As Zev Trachtenberg points out, Condorcet's results came out in 1785, twenty-three years after the *Social Contract*'s publication. Trachtenberg, *Making Citizens*, p. 281 n.8.

12 According to the jury theorem 'the probability that majority is correct (P_m) is given by the formula $v^{h-k}/(v^{h-k} + e^{h-k})$ where number of voters $= n = h + k$ where h is the number of voters in the majority, v is the probability that each voter will give the correct answer and e is the probability that each voter will give the wrong answer' Trachtenberg, *Making Citizens*, p. 281 n.6.

13 Note the very similar passage in Locke's *Second Treatise*, which also seems to grant the right of determining the extent to which individual rights shall be limited for the common good to the 'Legislative':

> But though Men when they enter into Society, give up the Equality, Liberty, and Executive Power they had in the State of Nature, into the hands of the Society, to be so far disposed of by the Leglislative as the good of the Society shall require; yet it being only with an intention in every one the better to preserve himself his Liberty and Property; ... the power of the Society, or the *Legislative* constituted by them, *can never be supposed to extend farther than the common good.*
>
> (Locke, *Second Treatise*: §131)

14 Lemay, 'Rousseau et la peine de mort à l'Assemblée constituante', pp. 29–40.

15 Montesquieu, *The Spirit of the Laws*, p. 1.

16 OC3: 294.

17 A good example of this approach is Mandle, 'Rousseauian Constructivism', pp. 545–62.

7

THE LAWGIVER, CULTURE AND MORALITY

(Book 2, Chs 7–12)

How will a blind multitude, which often does not know what it wills because it rarely knows what is good for it, carry out an undertaking as great, as difficult, as a system of legislation?

(2.6.10)

For men, as they become at least weary of irregular justling, and hewing one another, and desire with all their hearts, to conforme themselves into one firme and lasting edifice; so for want, both of the art of making fit Lawes, to square their actions by, and also of humility and patience, to suffer the rude and combersome points of their present greatnesse to be taken off, they cannot without the help of a very able Architect, be compiled, into any other than a crasie building, such as hardly lasting out their own time, must assuredly fall on the heads of their posterity.

(Hobbes, *Leviathan*, ch. 29, p. 221)

One of the most curious and apparently anomalous features of the *Social Contract* is the figure of the lawgiver or legislator whom Rousseau discusses in Book 2, Chapter 7. The lawgiver solves a problem at the centre of Rousseau's thought, but arguably does so at the cost of diminishing its plausibility. That problem is the problem of will formation: Rousseau wants to argue, as we have seen, that a legitimate state is one in which the people, exercising their general will, are sovereign. But the people, plucked from the state of nature – or, worse, from competitive social institutions – are not likely to be able to will the general will successfully. They lack the social spirit, the sense of genuine solidarity and commonality with others that comes only after living together within a set of common social institutions over a very long period of time. When the state is first formed, we have an agglomeration of individuals rather than a people and, given that such a group will almost certainly fail to recognise where their common interest lies, the state will most likely be doomed from the start. Even if the individuals *could* perceive the common interest, there would probably be insurmountable problems of *compliance*: citizens would be tempted to advance their short-term interests at the expense of the whole and since even well-disposed citizens are going to lack an assurance of the co-operative intentions of their fellows, the whole social edifice would quickly collapse. Accordingly, Rousseau makes room for a special individual to guide the people. The apparent role of this special individual is to enable the people to frame suitable laws, but he also has a secret task: that of moulding the people into a moral and cultural community.

The *Social Contract* is not the only one of Rousseau's works in which a lawgiver-like figure appears. In *Julie* we encounter the figure of Wolmar, the presiding genius of Clarens, and in *Emile* the figure of the tutor plays a similar role, transforming the pupil's self so that he can live an autonomous life in a world dominated by inflamed *amour propre*. Lawgivers appear as such both in the *Essay on the Origin of Languages* and in his *Considerations on the Government of Poland* and, both there, and in sketching a constitution for Corsica, Rousseau steps into the role himself. He also draws on a long tradition of writing about lawgiver-like figures, stretching from Plato's

The Statesman, through Bacon's *Essays*, Machiavelli's *Discourses* and Descartes' *Discourse on Method*. And we must add to that list the history and mythology of great lawgivers such as Lycurgus, the founder of Sparta, the Romans Numa and Solon, and religious leaders such as Moses, Mohammed and, of course, the architect of Rousseau's Geneva: Calvin.[1]

WHY THE LAWGIVER IS NEEDED

Rousseau is committed to the view that human character and motivation is largely shaped by social institutions. To be sure this is not the whole story: man is good by nature and social institutions have corrupted him. But he faces the difficulty of outlining a legitimate political order given 'men as they are' (1.0.1), that is men as they have emerged from history, men as they have been shaped by markets and hierarchies. Moreover, institutions may have corrupted man, but they also offer the solution to his troubles. As he puts it in Chapter 2 of the *Geneva Manuscript*, 'let us endeavour to derive from the evil itself the remedy which will cure it. By means of new associations, let us correct, if possible, the lack of a general association' (G2: 159/OC3: 288). In the *Social Contract* proper, the redeeming character of new institutions is plain in the 'remarkable change in man' which occurs in the transition to the civil state (1.8.1).

Institutions, then, while they may debase man and produce 'slaves contrary to nature' (1.2.8), also offer the possibility of unlocking and putting to work the natural goodness that they have historically suppressed. But if they offer that possibility, how are people to access it? It is a necessary condition for legitimate authority that citizens rule themselves, that they are not subject to the will of others. Nevertheless, they can only achieve this condition if they assume the role of citizens, subject to laws that they themselves have willed, laws applying impartially to all. Earlier in Book 2, Rousseau had given the impression that consideration of self-interest, subject to the constraint that the law that I will must apply in the same manner to all, would be sufficient to ensure that that general will emerges in the assembly (2.4.5). Contrary to this impression, there is good reason to believe that mere consideration of the interests that I have in common with others and of the best co-operative means to satisfy them will fail to provide the basis for a stable and enduring society and is an impoverished conception of what Rousseau had in mind.

We can see this by considering the deer hunters whom Rousseau discusses in the *Discourse on Inequality*. The deer hunters are quite capable of considering the concrete interests that they happen to hold in common with others and, indeed, of acting together with those others to satisfy and protect those interests. Even so, when temptation bounds past in the shape of a tasty rabbit and one hunter has the choice to satisfy his needs non-co-operatively, he will pursue self-interest at the expense of his fellow hunters. What the deer hunters lack is the kind of *shared* interest that can form the basis of an enduring common life together. Citizens who participate in common activities do not just partake of goods that they happen, as a matter of contingent fact, to value alongside their fellow citizens, they also come to value intrinsically collective goods: they dance and sing together and they come to attach intrinsic value to the commonality of that experience. (Sceptics about this, who are inclined to assimilate all such instances to cases of private enjoyment of goods might reflect on the difference between a relationship of friendship with another person, and a relationship with another person who just *acts* as a friend.) That mutually-valued commonality of identity and experience enables them in turn to sustain institutions which realise values of freedom, justice and equality. As Nannerl Keohane puts it:

> This shared commitment creates, and has for its object, a third type of common interest, resting on the other two, but more abstract and lofty. The convergence of particular ends, and the sharing of patriotic experiences, are necessary means to association; the third type of common interest is the goal. This includes those things in which citizens are most deeply interested: the enjoyment of liberty, the maintenance of equality, the institution of the rule of law.[2]

A just society requires that citizens have a certain conception of themselves and (crucially) of others: not only do they see themselves as pursuers of various goals, they also recognise others as doing the same and are willing to recognise those others as equally entitled to pursue their aims under a system of fair terms of co-operation. Citizens thus enjoy liberty to pursue their aims, subject to the equal right of others to do likewise under a publicly known system of co-operative conventions.[3]

The individuals who first associate together to form the state, however, though they perceive the need to work together to overcome the difficulties they face in common, lack the experience of shared life together that would lead them to attach an intrinsic value to their social and political arrangements. The shared knowledge that citizens have of the value that they each associate with the civil order gives each a firm guarantee of the co-operation of the others. But the first associates are not in that position; as Rousseau explains:

> For a nascent people to be capable of appreciating sound maxims of politics and of following the fundamental rules of reason of State, the effect would have had to become the cause, the social spirit which is to be the work of the institution would have to preside over the institution itself, and men would have to be prior to laws what they ought to become by means of them.
>
> (2.7.9)

The first associates are very much in the position of the deer hunters, or of the 'independent man' of the *Geneva Manuscript,* or of the individual from 1.7.7 who may be led 'to look on what he owes to the common cause as a gratuitous contribution'.

We have, then, two closely related problems: the first citizens are incapable of willing together a genuinely general will. What they decide together will not have the content that it needs if it is to form the basis for a stable and enduring polity and they are unlikely to be able to meet the most minimal demands of compliance with co-operative conventions (and will certainly fail to meet the threshold of assuring their putative fellow co-operators that they are reliable co-operative partners). Only on the basis of living together within just institutions would they acquire the co-operative dispositions that those institutions would need to subsist; only those who already had those dispositions would see the need for those very institutions. It looks as if we are in a circle from which there can be no escape. The lawgiver enables Rousseau to escape from that circle.

THE QUALITIES OF THE LAWGIVER

When Rousseau starts to enumerate the qualities the lawgiver must have in order to perform his task, it immediately becomes clear just how unlikely it is that this particular solution will be realised. The lawgiver, Rousseau tells us would have to be a person of:

> a superior intelligence who saw all of man's passions and experienced none of them, who had no relation to our nature yet knew it thoroughly, whose happiness was independent of us and who was nevertheless willing to care for ours; finally, one who, preparing his distant glory in the progress of times, could work in one century and enjoy the reward in another. It would require gods to give men laws.
>
> (2.7.1)

First, the lawgiver must know about the passions that animate man, especially *amour propre*, in order to judge successfully which laws correspond to our common interest. But, second, he must not be subject to those passions himself since if he were, he would have an interest in guiding the people to will institutions corresponding to his particular will (cf. 2.1.3). Third, insofar as the lawgiver does have passions, he must be content to satisfy them on a historical timescale, since his work can only be judged according to whether the institutions he designs persist and flourish over many generations.[4] The lawgiver is, then, 'an extraordinary man in the state' (2.7.4), and although he is so because of his role, he is also extraordinary because of his 'genius'. The need for this extraordinary genius creates a number of acute problems for Rousseau's theory, chief among which are the problem of where the lawgiver will come from, which we can call the 'regress problem' and the apparent inconsistency between Rousseau's assumption that citizens are to be regarded as free and equal and the granting of a natural superiority to the lawgiver: this we can call the problem of natural inequality.

THE REGRESS PROBLEM

An extraordinary genius is necessary if the state is to be properly formed, but where is it to be found? In the *Geneva Manuscript* Rousseau admits that this is a concern:

> The science of the Lawgiver is directed to this great object [the framing of laws ensuring the conservation of the state], but what is this science, where is the genius who possesses it to be found, and what virtues as necessary to the person who would dare to make us of it; this research is of great size and difficulty, and is even discouraging to anyone with pretensions to seeing the birth of a well-instituted state.
>
> (OC3: 312–13)

Indeed. Presumably the possessor of this science must be someone with experience of another polity, who has already been reshaped by participation in a political order. But if so, we encounter a problem of regress: how did the people of the lawgiver's native country get themselves guided to just laws? This difficulty of finding a superior intelligence to guide the people has an exact parallel in *Emile*, where Rousseau raises the difficulty of finding a tutor for his young pupil. As he puts it there:

> It would be necessary that the governor had been raised for his pupil . . . It would be necessary to go from education to education back to I know not where. How is it possible that a child be well raised by one who was not well raised himself? Is this rare mortal to be found? I do not know.
>
> (E1: 50/OC4: 263)

In the *Social Contract* it appears that, once again, he does not know. The problem is left forever unresolved.

Perhaps we can come to Rousseau's assistance here, at least to the extent of suggesting that each particular successful political foundation may not require a miracle. We know that Rousseau believes that particular peoples have to have tailor-made social institutions, but he leaves somewhat indeterminate the extent of the *variation* among constitutions. If well-ordered societies can be rather similar to one another, this will greatly reduce the need for extraordinary geniuses. New peoples can adopt or adapt the constitutions of other states, can learn from their successes and failures. Perhaps *some* genius is necessary to judge soundly the merits and demerits of other people's institutions, but it need not be the genius of Lycurgus; the (not inconsiderable, but still human) talents of Hamilton and Madison might do just as well. To the degree that knowledge of political affairs is cumulative and transmissible then, the task of founding a new political order becomes tractable. Rousseau himself, after all, draws on works of history and political theory and thereby builds on the experience of peoples and their lawgivers.

SUPERIOR INTELLIGENCE AND THE PROBLEM OF EQUALITY

Such a (partial) solution to the regress problem also mitigates the natural inequality problem. If most lawgivers do not need such extraordinary qualities after all, the problem that sharp differences in political competence poses for Rousseau's assumption of human equality will not be so great. But even granting the lawgiver such superhuman qualities may not be as damaging for Rousseau's political outlook as is sometimes thought.

The apparent difficulty is that the lawgiver's special qualities – including his 'superior intelligence' – seem to call into question Rousseau's rejection of natural aristocracy in 1.2. In that part of his argument he had seemed to reject 'Caligula's reasoning' according to which 'men are not naturally equal, but some were born for slavery and others for domination' (1.2.7). Here he refers to that reasoning again, saying that Plato in the *Statesman* reasons as to right, as Caligula had done as to fact.[5] The reference to Plato is instructive. In the *Statesman* the laws are really a second-best solution to the problem of social organisation. A truly superior genius would *not* rule according to law, since law, taking the form as it does of general laws applicable to all is always going to be somewhat insensitive to the moral requirements of particular cases. As the Visitor puts it in the *Statesman*:

> . . . law could never accurately embrace what is best and most just for all at the same time, and so prescribe what is best. For the dissimilarities between human beings and their actions, and the fact that practically nothing in human affairs ever remains stable, prevent any sort of expertise whatsoever from making a simple decision in any sphere that covers all cases and will last for all time.[6]

But, given the limitations of our human situation (the lack of such a superior genius), it is better to live (and to rule) according to fixed laws; and rulers who do not do so are not geniuses but tyrants who merely imitate the expert knowledge of the legislator but do not share it.

We can use Plato's thought here to reduce the tension between Rousseau's rejection of natural aristocracy as a theory of sovereignty and his suggestion that it is *necessary* for the lawgiver to be of a superior nature to the people. On one of the other occasions that Rousseau mentions Plato's discussion in the *Statesman*, he suggests that in evaluating monarchy as a form of government we have to look to how it will function under a range of monarchs with different abilities instead of thinking about how it might operate under the rare 'King by nature'.[7] A truly wise lawgiver, seeking to found a state that will endure over many generations, must design institutions on the assumption that *normal* conditions will prevail. He must take 'men as they are and laws as they can be'. Those normal conditions cannot include the assumption of the permanent presence of an extraordinary genius, but must take a rough and ready equality as given. Peoples will do much better being governed by settled and established laws than they would by relying on the qualities of exceptional individuals, especially as nearly all of those who pretend to such qualities do not, in fact, have them (usually such pretenders will turn out to be tyrants).

WHAT THE LAWGIVER DOES (AND DOES NOT) DO

Perhaps the first thing to stress about the lawgiver's role is that he does not have any legislative authority. Officially, the task of the lawgiver is to frame a system of laws that will serve as a constitutional framework for the new political order. It is for the people as a whole to ratify those laws.[8] 'Laws are, properly speaking, nothing but the conditions of the civil association' (2.6.10), they set out in the most general terms the way in which citizens are related to one another and to the sovereign (and crucially, as we shall see, they regulate the form of *government*). These laws are not ones that are applicable in all times and places but, rather, are tailored to specific peoples and circumstances: Rousseau sets out some of the causes of variation in the chapters immediately following 2.7. For a lawgiver to be able to do his work, first, the people must be suitable. Here are yet more obstacles in the way of a legitimate state. It seems as if peoples can only be reshaped when young: 'with age they grow incorrigible' (2.8.2). But only three paragraphs later he tells us that, 'there is a time of maturity for which one has to wait before subjecting them to laws' (2.8.5). Not too soon and not too late seems to be Rousseau's advice. He also allows that nations may undergo revolutionary crises, moments of collective amnesia, which make refoundation possible: but he warns that this can only happen once in the life of a people. Second, the state must be neither too large nor too small: a state that is too large is liable to be weighed down by excessive administration and its people are likely to see it as an abstract remote entity rather than being the expression of their general will. A state that is too small will not be self-sufficient and will fall prey to more powerful neighbours.

The focus on formal regulation gives a misleading impression of what the lawgiver's real work is all about. After setting out a three-fold classification of the laws (political, civil and criminal), Rousseau tells us that we must add a further category:

> . . . which is graven not in marble or bronze, but in the hearts of the Citizens; which is the State's genuine constitution; which daily gathers new force; which, when the other laws age or die out, revives or

replaces them, and imperceptibly substitutes the force of habit for that of authority. I speak of morals, customs, and above all of opinion; a part [of the laws] unknown to our politicians but on which the success of all the others depends: a part to which the great Lawgiver attends in secret, while he appears to restrict himself to particular regulations, which are but the ribs of the arch of which morals, slower to arise, in the end form the immovable Keystone.

(2.12.5)

In this passage, Rousseau makes clear that the real foundation of political success is cultural transformation and that the lawgiver's real task is to effect this. Naturally, this raises the issue of how this is to be done.

HOW THE LAWGIVER DOES WHAT HE DOES

Whether the lawgiver is framing regulations or inspiring moral change, a great obstacle to his work is the incapacity of the people to appreciate the reasons supporting his actions. Rousseau makes it very clear that the lawgiver cannot just try to persuade the people of the good reasons that support his legislative proposals. The people are cognitively ill-equipped to receive such reasons. Rather, the lawgiver must 'persuade without convincing' (2.7.9).

The distinction between persuading and convincing is an ancient one, going back at least to Aristotle. Kant employs the distinction when he writes: 'The touchstone whereby we decide whether holding a thing is true is conviction or mere persuasion is therefore external, namely, the possibility of communicating it and finding it to be valid for all human reason.'[9] Mere acts of persuasion do not generate beliefs in the same way that rational argument does: they are inherently local, tied to circumstance and context, to rationally irrelevant factors such as tone of voice or charismatic presence. Recently, postmodernists such as Derrida have denied the distinction between convincing and persuading: those convinced (or persuaded) by their argumentative (or rhetorical) strategies will have to remain unconvinced (or unpersuaded) by mine.[10]

The lawgiver must get people to act not by means of arguments establishing the rationality of their action, but rather by inspiring them, by the inflammation of their passions. Such persuasion will characteristically involve the use of religious symbols as well as music, games and ceremony.[11] These instruments need special skills if they are to be applied effectively. The lawgiver who aspires to getting the people to construct a long-lasting political order must have both charismatic authority and genuine wisdom. Rousseau tells us, perhaps rather implausibly, that 'Any man can carve tablets of stone, bribe an oracle, feign secret dealings with some divinity, train a bird to speak in his ear, or find other crude ways to impress the people' (2.7.11). But 'Empty tricks form only as passing bond'.

Interestingly, characteristics that are held up as virtues for the lawgiver, such as skilful oratory, are marked out as vices by Rousseau elsewhere in his work. In the *Discourse on Political Economy* he is scathing about 'eloquence' which is a tool used by skilful men to get the people to adopt what is, in fact, in the private interest of a few (G2: 16/OC3: 246). And in the *Social Contract* itself, Rousseau has the people of a well-constituted state:

> laugh as they imagine all the nonsense of which a clever knave or an insinuating talker could persuade the people of Paris or London. They do not know that Cromwell would have been condemned to hard labour by the people of Berne . . .
>
> (4.1.3)

The first associates presumably lack the political *nous* of the people of Berne and will be unable to tell the difference between a Lycurgus and a Cromwell. Does this matter? Perhaps not, since having these special persuasive powers is a necessary and not a sufficient condition for the lawgiver's success. Maybe an analogue of natural selection takes place: peoples who have the ill fortune to be founded by a Cromwell will simply not enjoy long-term political success.

In the *Social Contract* Rousseau is not particularly forthcoming about the details of the lawgiver's moral and cultural transformation of a people. In other works, notably the *Considerations on the Government of Poland*, he has more to say. Writing of the need to foster a spirit of patriotic unity he asks: 'How, then can one move hearts . . . Dare I say it? with children's games; with institutions which appear trivial in the eyes of superficial men, but which form cherished habits and invincible attachments' (G2: 179/OC3: 955). In the immediately following chapter, entitled 'Spirit of the Ancient Institutions', Rousseau discusses the three ancient lawgivers whom he thinks most worthy of attention: Moses, Lycurgus and Numa. He explains that they each sought to foment an emotional attachment between the individual and the *patrie* and that they used peculiarly national religious ceremonies, public games, and ceremonies reminding the people of the achievements of their ancestors in order to do this. (He explicitly refers the reader to the discussion of civil religion in the *Social Contract*.) He contrasts the Greeks with their public declamations of Homer, the public performances of Aeschylus, Sophocles and Euripides, and their sporting and athletic contests with the moderns whose religion does not attach them to their particular nation and whose entertainments are educations in vice. Music, with its unique ability to reach into the mind and elicit emotional response is a key part of this educative and transformative process. (Indeed, Rousseau suggests in his *Dictionary of Music* that in the ancient world even the transmission of the law was the business of song.)[12] Throughout Rousseau's work, music and dance are in the foreground of his account of what creates an affective community. To cite but one, well known example, perhaps the most striking single image of social unity and patriotic identification in Rousseau's work is the image of the dancing regiment from the *Letter to D'Alembert*.[13]

PERSUASION AND FREEDOM

The lawgiver's necessary reliance on techniques that work behind the back of citizens, his need to manipulate their desires rather than appealing to the good reasons that apply to them, creates an obvious difficulty concerning freedom. Although laws must be 'submitted to the free suffrage of the people' (2.7.7), so the people seem to choose the laws that are to govern their lives, the explanation for why they choose as they do is that the lawgiver has arranged matters so that they will. This parallels a particularly chilling passage in *Emile* where Rousseau discusses the way in which the tutor gets the pupil to obey him without commanding him directly:

> Let him always believe he is the master, and let it always be you who are. There is no subjection so perfect as that which keeps the appearance of freedom. Thus the will itself is made captive.
>
> (E2: 120/OC4 362)

If the will of the people is 'captive', if they then have merely the 'appearance of freedom', how can it *matter* whether or not they go through the motions of agreeing to the laws to which they are subject? And how can this count as an instance of their 'free suffrage'?

Perhaps we should not make too much of this. After all, there are many activities which require training and constraint before they can be engaged in freely and often the person being trained may not see the rationale for the exercises they undertake until they have become competent themselves. Thus, a person learning a musical instrument cannot just engage in music making from the beginning, but instead must practise scales and other exercises, must progress from easy pieces to ones of greater difficulty and must gradually develop sensitivity of touch and ear. So, perhaps similarly, citizens of a state at its very beginning, lacking the capacity for exercising the distinctive virtues of citizenship may need training and, indeed, transforming, before they can function properly as citizens of a democratic polity. John Stuart Mill – not normally accused of 'totalitarianism' – allows that nations in their 'nonage' may be subjected to the authority of superior wisdom.[14] What is problematic here, though, is less some 'totalitarianism' on Rousseau's part but, rather, his insistence on retaining the forms of republican legitimacy at a moment when they cannot have any genuine substance.

DENATURING

Rousseau's characterisation of what the lawgiver does with respect to human nature may also give cause for concern. In a passage that again parallels sections of *Emile*, Rousseau talks of 'transforming each individual who by himself is a perfect and solitary whole into part of a larger whole'; he must make it so that 'each Citizen is nothing and can do nothing except with all the others' (2.7.3). In *Emile* he had written:

> Natural man is entirely for himself. He is a numerical unity, the absolute whole which is relative only to itself or its kind. Civil man is only a fractional unity dependent on the denominator; his value is determined by his relation to the whole, which is the social body. Good social institutions are those that best know how to denature man, to take his absolute existence from him in order to give him a relative one and transport the *I* into the common unity, with the result that each individual believes himself no longer one but a part of the unity and no longer feels except within the whole.
>
> (E1: 39–40/OC4: 249)

It sounds as if Rousseau is advocating stripping the citizen of all individuality. But *that* would not achieve what Rousseau wants to achieve. The peasants whom Karl Marx famously likens to potatoes in a sack in his *Eighteenth Brumaire of Louis Bonaparte,* have identical forms of life to one another, but they just coexist side-by-side.[15] For Rousseau's citizens to become what he wants them to become, they have to be turned into functionally interdependent parts of a whole political order. This interdependence has at least two aspects: socio-economic and psychological. As soon as there is a developed division of labour within society individuals become dependent on the co-operation of others if their needs are to be met. But this co-operative interdependence is compatible with (indeed may engender) the most extreme individualistic attitudes.[16] Rousseau does not just want the fact of co-operative interdependence, he also wants this to be accompanied with a sense of team membership. In this respect the lawgiver is akin to a sports coach who gets the team to play better by transforming them from a rabble of individually talented but non-co-operating individuals into players with an 'all for one and one for all' spirit.

Is what Rousseau says here incompatible with a liberal concern for individual freedom? The first aspect of interdependence – the functional interdependence of citizens – had better be compatible with individual freedom if liberalism is to retain any plausibility, since that very functional interdependence will be a pervasive feature of all liberal societies. The team-spiritedness, or patriotism, that Rousseau calls for is slightly more problematic. Sometimes he appears to suggest that the good citizen has no aims or desires other than the good of the state. If he does say this, though, he is contradicting himself, since in Chapter 4 of the same book he says that 'in addition to the public person, we must consider the private persons who make it up, and whose life and freedom are naturally independent of it' (2.4.2). There, he suggests that individuals have a private sphere of interest and concern that lies alongside their public role as citizens. What we need to say here is that individuals come to value their status and role as citizens because of the way in which their assuming this co-equal role with others makes possible the substitution of justice for instinct (1.8.1). It is not that individuals have been psychologically absorbed into a whole; rather, it is that in assuming the identity of citizen, they willingly accept an obligation to 'regulate their conduct by principles that publicly can be justified to and accepted by their fellow citizens'.[17] Their 'denaturing' is an abandonment of interpersonal relationships based on relative physical or mental strength and an acceptance of the need to be bound by the law.

PSEUDOCHRONOLOGY

One further matter should detain us: what Rousseau has to say in the final chapters of Book 2 renders problematic the chronological account of the social pact that he seemed to presuppose in Book 1. The four chapters immediately following Rousseau's discussion of the lawgiver are a discussion of the human material that he has to deal with and the circumstances in which a state may be founded.

In Book 1, it looks very much as if the formation of the new political order by the social pact comes at the end of the long process of social degeneration that Rousseau charts elsewhere: most notably in the *Second Discourse*. The state of nature has turned, by degrees, into the Hobbesian war of all against all and self-interest leads individuals to enter into the social pact to preserve their lives and to secure civil liberty to replace the natural liberty that has become so precarious. In 1.5 Rousseau discusses the 'act by which a people is a people' which he says is the 'true foundation of society' (1.5.2). Yet it seems we must revise this picture since in Book 2 we find the lawgiver setting to work on a people which already exists. This suggests, perhaps, that the process by which an enduring civil order is founded may be gradual or be composed of several stages. This is consistent with what he says in *Poland*, where he contrasts the role of Numa with that of Romulus in the foundation of Rome. Numa he regards as the true lawgiver and founder. All Romulus had done was to 'assemble some brigands whom a reversal could scatter'. Numa had accomplished the truly important work by 'uniting these brigands into an indissoluble body, by transforming them into Citizens' (G2: 181/OC3: 957).

LEGITIMACY AND SOCIAL UNITY

What, then, should be the impact of these chapters on our understanding of the *Social Contract*? If we consider the circumstances of the first formation of the state, perhaps Rousseau believes the revolutionary moment of the social pact to be characterised by a sense of shared mission. To form a state successfully, individuals have to be capable of transcending the narrow standpoint of the neo-Hobbesian individual – the 'independent man' of the *Geneva Manuscript* – and the lawgiver helps them to do this by the fostering of festivals, games and so on. But there is a contrast between the 'revolutionary' and the normal. The power that is instituted by the social pact must – and inevitably does – become routinised. Jean Starobinski sees parallels between the moment of the social pact where '. . . each, by giving himself to all, gives himself to no-one' and the dancing regiment of the *Letter to D'Alembert*,[18] and it seems that there is something right about this: the lawgiver must indeed induce passions of unity and belonging in order to kick-start the commonwealth. Nevertheless, when Starobinski asserts 'The exaltation of the collective festival has the same structure as the general will of the Social Contract',[19] he is exaggerating the role of collective experience. The general will, for its successful operation requires both the commonality of citizenship and an awareness of one's separateness as an individual (2.4.5).

John T. Scott writes, 'For Rousseau, a legitimate state must rest upon an affective cultural basis: a community of shared mores, customs, and opinions.'[20] This is indeed right if he means to say that such an affective community is a necessary causal condition for the subsistence of a legitimate state. Cultural community, along with other factors such as a rough material equality is certainly among the background sociological conditions without which, Rousseau believes, the state must inevitably fail since its legitimacy will sooner or later be undermined by the de facto appropriation of what belongs to everyone – state power – by a subset of the population. But we should not draw the conclusion that such a community of shared mores is *constitutive* of the legitimacy of the state. A state is legitimate if the people exercise sovereignty through the expression of their general will; and for that to happen it must be the case that individuals come to be capable of reasoning together as citizens. The formation and maintenance of that identity to a degree that is sufficient for it to dominate the other identities citizens have in their practical collective deliberations is part of the work of the lawgiver and is sustained through public festivals, through song and dance. But though it forms that identity causally, it does not constitute it, it is not part of the meaning of what it is to be a citizen.

The ideal state combines individual autonomy and partial privacy on the one hand, with affective unity, a sense of commonality and patriotism on the other. Each of these two elements needs the other: individualism without community results in the triumph of the 'will of all' over the general will and the self-defeating competition of inflamed *amour propre*. Conversely, community without individualism would mean the engulfment of the individual in society and the loss of moral responsibility. While Rousseau may celebrate the social unity of the golden age, of the Greek polis or the self-sacrificing patriotism of Rome or Sparta, the state envisaged by the *Social Contract* is not the recreation in modern times of any of those images. All of them express components of Rousseau's conception of the good life, but all are both unrecoverable for moderns and, in any case, do not sum up all that Rousseau values. The dancing regiment of St Gervais expresses and builds the commonality of Geneva and, as such, makes a free society a possibility. But the soldiers do not dance unceasingly: there is a time for dancing and a time for individuals to reason together in common as citizens.

NOTES

1 Elsewhere, notably in the *Letters from the Mountain*, Rousseau revises his estimate of Calvin: 'Calvin was undoubtedly a great man; but he was in the end a man, and sorry to say, a Theologian' (OC3: 715).

2 Keohane, *Philosophy and the State in France*, pp. 441–2.

3 Many will see, rightly I think, a prefiguring of Rawls's conception of persons as free and equal in their possession of two characteristic moral powers: first, the capacity to frame, pursue and revise a conception of the good and second, the willingness to co-operate with others on fair terms (the sense of justice). For discussion of such Rousseauian prefiguring of Rawls see Mandle, 'Rousseauian Constructivism', pp. 545–62.

4 One is reminded of Zhou Enlai's remark when asked whether the French Revolution had been successful: 'It is too early to say'.

5 He will return to Caligula's position again in 4.8.1, where he suggests that at least a belief in the natural superiority of the ruler is necessary if the first peoples are to accept any kind of rule at all, and Plato's claim that there can be naturally superior kings is implicitly endorsed at 3.6.14 (if only to point out how unlikely they are).

6 *Statesman*, 294b, in Plato, *Complete Works*.

7 At 3.6.15.

8 This marks a sharp divide between Machiavelli and Rousseau. Cf. *Discourses*, I. IX, 'A sagacious legislator of a republic, therefore, whose object is to promote the public good, and not his private interests, and who prefers the country to his own successors, should concentrate all authority in himself'. Machiavelli, *The Prince and the Discourses*, p. 138.

9 Kant, *Critique of Pure Reason*, A820/B848.
10 I take it that the possibility of using language persuasively is, in fact, parasitic upon the use of language to make true statements about the world. This may not, though, have been Rousseau's view. In the *Essay on the Origin of Languages* Rousseau claims that figurative meaning preceded literal meaning (ch.3) and argues that the telos of the first languages was to communicate affect rather than information.
11 Machiavelli, *Discourses*, I. XI:

> In truth, there never was an remarkable lawgiver amongst any people who did not resort to divine authority, as otherwise his laws would not have been accepted by the people; for there are many good laws, the importance of which is known to the sagacious lawgiver, but the reasons for which are not sufficiently evident to enable him to persuade others to submit to them; and therefore do wise men, for the purpose of removing this difficulty, resort to divine authority.
>
> (p. 147)

12 See the entries for 'Music' and 'Chanson' in *Dictionary of Music* in *The Collected Writings of Rousseau vol. 7*, pp. 442 and 561n (OC5: 921 and 690).
13 In his *Essay on the Origin of Languages*, Rousseau seems to put cultural transformation forever beyond the reach of modern peoples (and certainly of French-speaking ones) with his insistence that the 'languages of the north' are inherently unsuitable for persuasion. See Christopher Bertram, 'Language, Music and the Transparent Society'.
14 Mill, 'On Liberty', in *'On Liberty' and Other Writings*, p. 13.
15 Marx, *Surveys from Exile*, p. 239.
16 Such as, perhaps, the libertarianism of an Ayn Rand, a Murray Rothbard or a Robert Nozick.
17 Mandle, 'Rousseauian Constructivism', p. 560.
18 See Starobinski, *Jean-Jacques Rousseau*, p. 121.
19 Ibid., p. 120.
20 Scott, 'Rousseau and the Melodious Language of Freedom', p. 803.

8

GOVERNMENT
AND SOVEREIGN

(Book 3)

One of Rousseau's central theoretical innovations is his distinction between government and sovereign. Book 3 of the *Social Contract* is largely devoted to an exploration of the distinction between these two bodies and the relationship between them. He argues that although sovereign power is always vested in the people, the power to execute, administer and interpret the laws should be placed in a special body, the government, composed of figures he calls 'magistrates'. The proper relationship between sovereign, government and individual is central to the well-ordering of political society and is one of the objects of the lawgiver's art. Although the practical problem of institutional design is at the centre of Rousseau's concerns in Book 3, he also uses the opportunity to give vent to his radical pessimism concerning the durability of human institutions. Even the best constructed of polities is bound to fail eventually and to see the sovereign power snatched from those who ought to hold it – the people – and placed in the hands of a clique.

In this chapter I focus on the problem that Rousseau has at the centre of his theory of institutional design, namely getting the right balance between, on the one hand, the 'rectitude' of the state (its conformity with the general will) and, on the other, its capacity to direct the common force of all the citizens effectively in accordance with that will. Not only must institutions be designed in such a way that the general will emerges reliably from their operation, if it is not to remain a dead letter, it also has to be possible to get everyone to act as the general will decides. If citizens are perfectly virtuous and well-informed, if they have a strong sense of belonging to the community, it will be easy to get them to conform to the general will. But to the extent to which citizens are alienated from the community and their fellows, there will be a problem about getting them to obey the general will (even when they can still formulate and recognise that will) when their particular will has more salience for them. If we need a body to implement, interpret and enforce the general will, a danger will arise that that body will form and pursue, not the general will, but its own will. It is the old issue: 'Sed quis custodiet ipsos Custodes?'.[1]

THE GOVERNMENT AND ITS TASK (3.1.1–7)

Before addressing the substantive issues, Rousseau has to clarify some terminology. He begins Book 3 by telling us that his preliminary purpose is definitional: he wants to fix the precise meaning of the term 'government'. But he also tells us that this is not going to be an easy ride, that his chapter on 'Government in General' (3.1) needs to be read carefully and attentively. He starts his discussion by running one of his favourite analogies: that between the human body and the body politic. Actions have two causes: moral and physical. There must be a concurrence of these two elements for any action to be performed successfully. A person who lacks the will to rise from his bed and walk will not be able to do so; a person whose limbs are paralysed cannot do so either. In the body politic we have a similar distinction between the will to perform an action, which Rousseau calls legislative power, and the power to carry it out, which he calls executive power. Rousseau tells us that 'Nothing is or should be done in the body politic without their concurrence' (3.1.2).

Developing the principles already established in Books 1 and 2, Rousseau reminds us that this legislative power can and should only belong to the people as a whole. By contrast, the people cannot, at least as sovereign, exercise executive power. This is because, as Rousseau has been at pains to explain in Book 2, the general will is always general 'in its object and its essence' (2.4.5). However, for executive power to be exercised the state needs to direct its attention to particular objects, to the question of whether this or that action conforms to the law, rather than to the content of the law in general.

As we shall see, the carrying out of this executive power does not, strictly speaking, require a separate body. All the citizens could, should they so choose, be the agents executing their own will. Rousseau worries, though, that in attending to particular cases the citizen body will become corrupt. 'Hard cases make bad law', the saying goes, and if they fail to start from the standpoint of generality but, rather, seek to frame laws to deal with particular cases and interests, citizens will lose the capacity for detachment and impartiality.[2] Rousseau's sharp separation between the business of legislation and matters of interpretation and enforcement would seem, though, to be indefensible and naïve. It is a commonplace that judges *make* law in the process of interpreting it and, indeed, it is hard to see how any body charged with implementation, interpretation and enforcement could do otherwise.[3]

What is this body exercising executive power? It is the government. The government 'serves as a means of communication between the State and the Sovereign' (3.1.4), it is the agent which unites and puts to work the public force 'in accordance with the directives of the general will' (3.1.4), it is 'an intermediate body established between subjects and Sovereign' (3.1.5). Its tasks include the execution of the laws and the maintenance of both the exercise of political liberties by citizens and their individual liberty vis-à-vis the state and one another (3.1.5). In addition to *the* government, the specific body which undertakes these tasks, Rousseau also writes of the *task* of government which he defines as the 'legitimate exercise of the executive power' (3.1.7). The government, which Rousseau also calls the Prince, is composed of individuals who bear the title 'magistrate'. Rousseau is clear that they are merely the agents of the sovereign, they are doing a job on the sovereign's behalf and the sovereign can dismiss them or alter the terms under which they do their jobs. To that extent, their relationship to the political community is similar to that of Locke's government in his *Second Treatise*, it is a relationship of trust which can, in principle be revoked.[4]

ROUSSEAU'S MATHEMATICAL ANALOGIES (3.1–2)

Rousseau attempts to illustrate the relationships that obtain between sovereign, government and subjects in terms of mathematical relations and ratios. This can seem somewhat odd to the modern reader, not to mention being confusing and perplexing. He tells us that the relation between the Sovereign and the State (i.e. between the political community as a deliberating and legislating body on the one hand and the aggregation of individuals who are subject to the law on the other) can be represented as 'the ratio between the extremes of a continued proportion of which the mean proportional is the Government'. A proportion is a relationship between terms such that A is to B as C is to D. So, for example, 1 is to 2 as 4 is to 8. In this example, the extremes (A and D) are 1 and 8, and B and C (2 and 4, respectively) are the 'means'. The proportion is said to be 'continued' if the second term (its consequent) of the first ratio is either equal to the first term of the second ratio (its antecedent) or, alternatively if the ratio between these two terms (B and C) is the same as the ratios between A and B and between C and D. In the case where the consequent of the first ratio is equal to the antecedent of the second, we have, effectively three terms (call them P, Q and R) and two ratios $P:Q$ and $Q:R$, where $P/Q = Q/R$. Here, the product of the extremes ($P \times R$) is equal to the product of the means (here $Q \times Q$), giving rise to the relation $P \times R = Q^2$. Q is the 'mean proportional' between the two extremes.[5]

Rousseau tries to explain the application of this idea by means of a numerical example. If we take a state with 10,000 citizens, we can consider those individual persons under two aspects. On the one hand, they are members of a sovereign collective body to which we can assign a force equal to that of the population as a whole (10,000). On the other hand, as individuals subject to the law that they themselves have passed, they each count as one. If we increase the population tenfold, the individual remains just as subject to the law, but it is a law that he has a greatly (tenfold) diminished role in making. In other words, as the state increases in size, the individual has a greatly diminished sense of 'ownership' of that state, his vote has increasingly less chance of affecting the outcome of a vote, and the laws appear more and more to him as an alien power outside of his control rather than as the expression of what he has willed in common with his fellow citizens. This growing sense of dissociation and alienation from the collective means that citizens are less and less likely spontaneously to comply with the common good, the general will appears to them more and more as an abstraction, divorced from their immediate interests. Accordingly, to get them to comply with the law, more repressive force and the threat of such force is needed, and governments must be given more power (3.1.12–13).

But the increased size, and hence power, of the state also places new temptations in the hands of the magistrates who make up the government. Accordingly, Rousseau tells us that as the relative force available to the magistrates to enforce the law on the individual subject increases (as it has to), the more relative force the people as sovereign also has to have to keep the magistrates from exceeding their proper power.

Since the relationship between sovereign, government and subjects takes the form of a continuous proportion in which one of the extremes is always one, it follows that the size of the government should always be the square root of the size of the sovereign. Rousseau worries that putting things in this too-neat form will expose him to ridicule. He tells us that he is 'using this number only as an example' and that 'the ratios about which I am speaking are measured not only by numbers of men, but more generally by the amount of activity' (3.1.16). This refers us back to 2.10.1 where he discusses some of the factors that bear of the force of the state. He argues there that there has to be an appropriate ratio between the population and the extent of the territory and that it is impossible to provide any general formula for this because of differences in such factors as climate and fertility of the soil. It would seem to follow from all this that Rousseau believes that while the 'square root' formula gives us a rule of thumb for the appropriate size of government, this can never be mechanically determined and will vary greatly depending on these further factors. Presumably, part of the art of the lawgiver is to design a relationship between government and sovereign that is appropriate given these variations. One of the lessons that he wants us to draw, is that there is no set of institutions that is applicable to all peoples and at all times, but that the crucial tasks of formulating the general will, getting the laws executed and subordinating the magistrates to the sovereign will require different solutions depending on circumstances.

It is the achievement of a balance between the subordination of the government to the sovereign and granting the government enough power to do its work effectively that occupies Rousseau from 3.1.17–22. The government must have an internal structure and subordinate bodies of its own and these pose similar problems for it to those which the existence of the government present for the sovereign. Rousseau suggests that similar proportional relationships arise between the government as a whole and individual magistrates as had arisen between sovereign and subjects and that intermediate bodies within the government itself should obey the same law of continued proportion as govern the size of the government itself: 'The difficulties arise in ordering this subordinate whole within the whole' (3.1.20).

One of the factors guiding Rousseau here is a view about the total force of the state. Though this will vary depending on population, territory and productivity, Rousseau takes it that there is a fixed stock of resource which is available to the body politic and which may be used for purposes including the execution of the laws by the magistrates and the control of individual magistrates by the government acting collectively. Rousseau explained in 3.1 that the larger the state, the increased alienation of the subject from the law and the greater the need for repressive force. Similarly, the larger the government the more the individual magistrates will disidentify from their common purpose and the more force will have to be expended on internal policing within the government. As a result, the government as a collective whole will be weaker due to the waste of part of the stock of force.

Rousseau tries to clarify matters for us by telling us that magistrates have, as it were, three wills (3.2.5). First, as private citizens they have particular wills that look to their own advantage. Second, as magistrates they have a will that is general in relation to the collective they form together (the government) and which expresses the common interest of that body. Third, they share the general will that looks to the common interest of the political community as a whole. Ideally, the general will expressed by the sovereign in legislation should be dominant over the corporate will of the magistrates and the particular will of individuals. But 'According to the natural order' (3.2.7) the various wills become more active according to how 'concentrated' they are. In a small, self-governing community with economic equality and closely shared morals (cf. 4.1.1), there is little difference between the particular will of individuals and the general will. Each person in such a community finds it easy to reason in common with others and has no special difficulty about grasping where shared interests lie. Identification with one's fellow citizens is very immediate and concrete. At the opposite extreme, expressed by Rousseau in his exploration of 'The General Society of the Human Race', common interests and identification with others are just intellectual abstractions which have no power to move individuals to action. In a small state, the concrete 'we' will have such practical force and obviousness that morals can largely take the place of laws and the government need not be strong (and magistrates can thus be numerous). In a large state, where social relationships have become nearly anonymous, the concrete 'we' hardly exists and our particular self-interested wills are concentrated and have a practical immediacy for us. In consequence, in such a large state, we need a small and decisive group of magistrates to execute the laws. But the more these magistrates form a small cabal, the more their corporate will as magistrates will be concentrated and it, too, will have a practical immediacy for them which will tend to overpower the general will (which will be as weak in the magistrates as it is in their fellow citizens).

Rousseau illustrates these relationships between wills and the public force by considering polar opposite cases. If we give the government to a single individual the corporate will of the magistracy will be as concentrated as it possibly can be. There is not even a single other person with whom this individual must deliberate in order to determine how to act. They will be able to act decisively and powerfully, since they have the whole public force at their disposal. At the opposite extreme, we could make everyone a magistrate. In this case the common identity of magistrates is the same as the common identity of citizens: the corporate will and the general will become one. The total stock of force available to the state is the same as ever but we will have a problem if we wish to direct it so as to ensure the execution of the laws. The problem is one of regress: we need to get people to act in common. Normally that is the job of the government, but here everyone is the government, so to get people to act in common, we would have already had to get them to act together! If everyone is the government, government is *relatively* weakest.

Some further considerations also influence Rousseau's view of the basic relationship between government and sovereign. First, the individual decision of the magistrate has far more bearing on the conduct of government than that of the citizen has on the sovereign. Not only is the magistrate active in government on a daily basis, whereas the citizen is usually not assembled with his fellow citizens as sovereign, but also the magistrate has probably been given some delegated function of government.

The two paragraphs at 3.2.12–13 need to be read together to get Rousseau's sense; taken separately they can be highly misleading. In 3.2.12, he addressed the question of governmental force and its desirable extent. Here, his emphasis is again on the need to increase the relative force of the government in order to combat the growing alienation of the citizens as the state grows in size. He tells us that the ratio of magistrates to government should be the inverse of the ratio of subjects to sovereign. It seems, then, as if Rousseau is advocating a *fall* in the absolute numbers of magistrates as the population grows. Needless to say, this would conflict with the 'continuous proportion' rule-of-thumb which requires the number of magistrates to *grow* in absolute terms while forming an ever smaller proportion of the total population. However, when we look at 3.2.13 we see that he has only been looking at one side of the question, since we need to balance the need for the government to have *force* with the need for it to maintain its *rectitude* (i.e. its propensity to govern in accordance with the will of the sovereign, the general will). As he has established already (e.g. at 3.2.9), as the number of magistrates becomes a larger proportion of the population, their corporate will tends to approximate the general will. It is, he tells us, the lawgiver's task to work out, for a particular political community, how to balance these conflicting *desiderata*. The continuous proportion rule represents a compromise between the competing demands of force and will.

THE FORMS OF GOVERNMENT (3.3)

Book 3 Chapter 3 is a brief transitional chapter in which Rousseau repeats the classical classification of governments into democracy, aristocracy and monarchy, using a purely numerical criterion. Democracy is the government of the many, aristocracy of the few and monarchy of just one supreme magistrate. Rousseau's adoption of this traditional schema is misleading in at least one respect: the traditional view distinguished among different forms of law-making body, whereas Rousseau, of course, restricts the law-making function to the political community as a whole. As he puts it at 2.6.9 'Every legitimate Government is republican', adding in a note:

> By this word I understand not only an Aristocracy or a Democracy, but in general any government guided by the general will, which is the law. To be legitimate the Government must not be confused with the Sovereign, but be its minister: Then monarchy itself is a republic.

Following the principles already established in 3.1 and 3.2, Rousseau takes the view that there is no single best form of government but that different constitutions suit different peoples and, at least this is his official view, 'each one of them is the best in some cases and the worst in others' (3.3.7). We shall see, though, that he is unenthusiastic in practice about the possibility of either democratic or monarchical government, for him these remain principally theoretical curiosities.

DEMOCRACY AS A FORM OF GOVERNMENT (3.4)

Rousseau begins his discussion of democracy by observing that one might think democracy to be obviously the best form of government since the people who make the laws ought to be the best judges of how to execute and interpret them (3.4.1). But, in fact, he believes this to be a flaw. The general will comes from all and applies to all (2.4.5) and if the people considers not just general principles but particular decisions, its ability to attend impartially to general principles will become impaired. What Rousseau seems to have in mind here is the thought that if the citizens were to govern directly, they would often be involved in judging in cases where their own private interests were involved and would therefore be susceptible to the same distortions of judgement that normally occur in such cases. Of course, magistrates might be tempted in the same way, but at least they are subject to a superior authority (that of the people) whereas in a state where all, or nearly all, govern directly there would be no such check on abuse and corruption.[6]

Democracy is, in any case, he thinks, rather an impractical form of administration given the demands it places on citizens. He writes that 'It is unimaginable that the people remain constantly assembled to attend to public affairs' (3.4.3). Yet Rousseau will soon tell us that in ancient Rome 'few weeks went by when the Roman people was not assembled, and even several times' (3.12.4) and in ancient Greece the people was 'constantly assembled in the public square' (3.15.9). So what appears 'unimaginable' at one moment appears to be historical fact at another. The difficulties and anomalies are compounded when we read at 3.4.5 of the background conditions that are required for the democratic form of government to function. Rousseau mentions three: a small state where the citizens know one another and are easily assembled. Second, a rough equality both of wealth and status. Third, an absence of 'luxury' which inevitably gives rise to selfishness, 'laxity' and vanity. As Richard Fralin has observed,[7] each of these characteristics is also put forward in the *Dedication* to the *Discourse on Inequality* as part of a description of eighteenth-century Geneva. Even if we agree with Helena Rosenblatt that such a description is laced with a heavy dose of irony, Rousseau is, at the very least, sketching an attainable ideal that Geneva falls short of. And if we look again at 3.15.12, we find him setting out smallness of size as a necessary condition for sovereign power itself to subsist.

It looks, then, as if we should substantially discount these objections based on impracticality and instead focus on the lack of fit between the task of government and the moral potentialities of the citizen. He has already told us of how dealing in particular matters will corrupt the judgement of citizens, at the end of the chapter he stresses Montesquieu's requirement that citizens of democracies be virtuous and writes 'If there were a people of Gods, they would govern themselves democratically' (3.4.8). This suggests that self-government would require a combination of knowledge, wisdom and virtue that is beyond the capacity of ordinary individuals (presumably even those inspired by the lawgiver). Will any other form of government prove less demanding?

ARISTOCRACY AS A FORM OF GOVERNMENT (3.5)

The second form of government Rousseau considers is *aristocracy*. Along with popular sovereignty, Rousseau was to claim later that the second principle established in the *Social Contract* was that aristocracy was the best form of government.[8] He distinguishes three different kinds: natural, elective and hereditary. Natural aristocracy, rejected as a form of *sovereign* power at 1.2, is seen as the original form of *government* at 3.5.2. Here, Rousseau is thinking of natural deference to established leaders, usually blood-relatives, in simple tribal societies. Although he clearly believes that this form of government can be a good one, it is unlikely to be best for societies that are somewhat more developed and complex. Hereditary aristocracy he describes as the 'worst of all Governments' (3.5.4): it is the culmination of a process of historical degeneration issuing in the emergence of a patrician class who are not likely to be suited to the job of governing.

The best form of government is 'elective aristocracy'. In this form, a small subset of the population are chosen on the grounds of their 'probity, enlightenment, experience and all the other reasons for public preferment' (3.5.5). The 'wise govern the multitude' (3.5.7), which Rousseau describes as the natural order of things. Other factors also work in favour of this form: a small assembly of people is easier to convene than a large one and business is carried on more efficiently. Rousseau clearly entertains the hope that a group of wise citizens will be able to rise above the consideration of their narrowly defined private interest and to take on the perspective of the public. Here again, there is inevitably compromise, since with anything less than the purest civic virtue, 'the corporate will begins to guide the public force less in accordance with the standards of the general will'. So aristocracy is always pregnant with oligarchic possibility: a small group of people governing the many may well be a consequence of the natural order of things, but they will need to be kept in check since their natural affections will lead them to try to convert elective aristocracy into a hereditary form of government unless the law clearly prescribes the form of election. Moreover, this is inevitably an inegalitarian form of government: the magistrates are to be freed from the necessity of work so as to permit them to give all their attention to the business of administration.

Rousseau's preferred form of government, then, depending on the details of how he expects it to work, suggests an intriguing closeness to modern representative government. To be sure, Rousseau is famous for rejecting the representation of *sovereignty*, but if lawmaking is confined to constitutional essentials and much of the detail of day to day government is a matter of decrees issued by a group of elected officials, the difference between the two models is appreciably diminished.[9]

MONARCHY AS A FORM OF GOVERNMENT (3.6)

Finally, Rousseau looks at monarchy. Although popular sovereignty is, in principle, consistent with monarchy as a form of government, what he actually says about government by a single man is overwhelmingly negative.

But he concedes that monarchy has at least this in its favour: it is *efficient*. Since the person charged with executing the popular will and the will of the government is the same natural individual, this is a form of government free of inner conflict. The business of government will not be held up by inner dissension or interminable delay but will be quick, efficient and decisive. At least that is Rousseau's view: he seems not to have considered the possibility that the natural individual in charge might be a hopeless procrastinator or someone pathologically incapable of knowing their own mind. But even though he believes that monarchy will be the most vigorous form of government (3.6.4), Rousseau thinks that kings will almost inevitably use their hold on government to subvert the authority of the sovereign and will not reliably pursue the public good.

In saying this, Rousseau is dissenting from Hobbes who had argued that a king's best interests lie in a contented and flourishing populace, able to defend the land against foreign enemies.[10] This possibility is rejected by Rousseau, who suggests that monarchs care far more about keeping subjects in their place. He mentions approvingly Machiavelli's provocative claim in *The Prince* that to rule by fear is more efficient than to flatter one's subjects: 'While pretending to teach lessons to Kings, he taught great lessons to peoples. Machiavelli's *Prince* is the book of republicans' (3.6.5).

Even in the absence of malicious intent by the king, monarchy still has almost insurmountable defects for Rousseau. According to the various ratios he laid out to regulate the government–sovereign relationship, monarchy is only suited to very large states, but although the concentration of public force in the hands of a single person may maximise decisiveness, it also presents formidable cognitive obstacles. The king cannot see what is going on everywhere at all times, nor can he possibly take all the decisions that must be taken, hence a need for delegation. So we begin to have a form of government that more and more resembles aristocracy, but with a crucial difference. Whereas in (elective) aristocracy, the principle of 'careers open to talents' applies – to use John Rawls's phrase – in a monarchy those who achieve administrative office are 'most often nothing but petty bunglers, petty knaves, petty schemers whose petty talents, which at Court give access to high places, only serve to show the public their ineptitude just as soon as they have acceded to these high places' (3.6.8). Again, Rousseau does not provide any evidence to support this claim, and some might think that democracies and aristocracies are as vulnerable to demagogues who flatter the people as monarchies are at the mercy of those who flatter kings.

In addition to these numerous defects, Rousseau also emphasises the problems of succession that arrive in a monarchy. If the succession is elective then the death of one king results in quarrel and dissension; if the principle is hereditary then we are subject to chance and fate: we may well end up with a psychopath or an imbecile. The government of the state is liable to abrupt swings and shifts depending on the character of the individual who happens to be on the throne at a particular moment. A polity that well-suits the temperament and intelligence of one individual may not suit the next.

Rousseau's hostility to monarchy as a form of government is evident in almost every line of his discussion. What is somewhat curious and unexplained is his lack of attention to the specific problem that he is officially addressing. When he attacks monarchy on the ground of experience and historical record, he is drawing on the familiarity of his readers with monarchy as a form of *sovereignty*. The Hobbesian argument that he implicitly attacks is also a discussion of monarchical *sovereignty* and it is clear that Machiavelli was not considering matters in the light of Rousseau's (later) government–sovereign distinction. No doubt Rousseau believes that monarchical government will so quickly usurp the sovereign power of the people and will so soon cease to rule in the public interest that the historical experience remains to the point.

MIXED FORMS (3.7)

Having given an exposition of the three classical forms of government, Rousseau now proceeds (3.7) to muddy the waters a little, by pointing out that every system of government is actually complex. Any large organisation, such as a government has to have systems of delegation, of division of labour and so on. The crucial point that he wants to insist upon is that the relationship between sovereign, government and subjects must be properly ordered. If the government is too weak in relation to the subjects then we can expect a high degree of criminality and disorder, if it is too strong towards the sovereign then we will see a subversion of the general will of the people in favour of the corporate will of the magistrates. Rousseau canvasses 'mixed government' – that is, a government composed of interdependent institutions – as a pragmatic remedy in the case where the size of the state necessitates a proportionally smaller government (hence more decisive and efficient) in order to compensate for the diminution of moral community among the citizens. The danger here, of course, is that popular sovereignty will be usurped by the magistrates. Division of the government will mean that 'its several parts have no less authority over the subjects, and their division reduces their combined force against the Sovereign' (3.7.4). But it is hard to see how this remedy will be effective, since presumably the appearance of inner division in the government would, *contra* Rousseau, plausibly result in a loss of authority over the subjects. There is also the possibility of *strengthening* the government through division. This can be applied in democratic governments where the problem is less a worry about the government subverting the general will in favour of its own independent interests, than it is about a lack of effective administration. Here, particular governmental functions can be delegated by the citizenry as a whole to particular individuals and committees. What we have in this case is a dilution of democratic government and its transformation into a form of elective aristocracy.

GEOGRAPHICAL DETERMINISM? (3.8–9)

Chapters 8 and 9 of Book 3 now appear even more quaint than the rest of Rousseau's writings on government. We already know that the size of a state is a crucial determinant of its form of government. Now Rousseau seeks to invoke general climatic conditions as well: 'Freedom, not being a fruit of every Clime, is not within the reach of every people' (3.8.1). Here we have yet another reminder of the problematic pseudochronology that lurks in the *Social Contract*. In 1.5.2, opposing Grotius, Rousseau had declared the social contract to be the act whereby a people constitutes itself as a people. But here, again, it is plain that a people can count as a people without establishing republican institutions.

So which climes should we expect to give rise to free institutions? This is a problem to which Rousseau had already given some thought. In the *Essay on the Origin of Languages* he had contrasted the languages of the north, which derived from harsh and guttural cries for help with the languages of the south – half-sung languages of love and sensuality. There he had declared that not only were the languages of the north inherently unmusical, they were also unfit for free peoples. The languages of the north were fit only for command and machination, but not for pronouncing a discourse in the public square.

One might, then, expect Rousseau to favour hot countries as seats of free institutions, with somewhere like Arabia (source of one of the archetypal languages of freedom) particularly favoured. But Rousseau tells us that 'in terms of the effect of climate, despotism suits warm countries, barbarism cold countries, and good polity intermediate regions'. Almost the whole emphasis in the *Social Contract* is, in fact, on the natural fertility of the soil and the effect of this on the relation between peoples and governments.

All governments live off the efforts of the people, but some are by nature frugal whereas others consume vast quantities. Democracies are hardly distinct from the people themselves and so they represent a very small charge on the people. Monarchies, with their retinues of courtiers and lackeys are expensive and burden-some. Some lands are so barren that they hardly support anything that merits the title of political organisation at all. Such are the peoples he describes as savage or barbarous. By contrast, extremely productive lands should be governed monarchically 'so that the Prince's luxury might consume the excess of the subjects' surplus; for it is better that this excess be consumed by the government than squandered by private individuals' (3.8.7). As Hilail Gildin has pointed out, this is a very rare instance of Rousseau having something positive to say about a despotic form of government.[11] The countries best suited to free government will, then, be those producing a moderate surplus: a great excess will force us to choose between a corrupt and effete people and a monarchy. In his *Project for a Constitution for Corsica* (1765), Rousseau suggests that the form of government a people gets is pretty much a function of the fertility of the soil and, speaking of Switzerland, he writes:

> Switzerland is generally a poor and sterile country. Her government is everywhere republican. But in those cantons that are more fertile than others, such as Berne, Soleure, and Fribourg, the government is aristocratic. In the poorest ones, where cultivation is the least rewarding and requires the most work, the government is democratic. The state there has only just enough to subsist under the simplest of administrations. It would exhaust itself and perish under any other.
>
> (OC3: 906)

It seems as if Rousseau is piling up the obstacles against the possibility of establishing free institutions. Free institutions are republican, that is, they are ones in which the people are actively sovereign. Their form of government is either going to be democratic – but as we have seen that demands an almost impossibly high standard of virtue for citizens – or there must be an elective aristocracy. But even in the case of elective aristocracy, the citizens must be virtuous if they are successfully to invigilate the operations of government. Too much excess, too much luxury is a threat to virtue and inevitably brings moral corruption.

When we see in 3.9, the principle by which political success may be judged, the picture becomes even bleaker! 'What is the aim of political association?', Rousseau writes, 'It is the preservation and prosperity of its members. And what is the surest sign that they are preserving themselves and prospering? It is their number and population.' But we already know the effects of increasing the size of the state. Each person will find their own voice increasingly diluted within the sovereign body; each person will come to see the state as increasingly alien to them. The social bond will slacken and the degeneration of the state will set in. It seems as if Rousseau has set up a natural dialectic of political development which will condemn even the most successful states on the ground of their very success. Permanence is a vain hope, relative durability is the best that can be achieved: 'If Sparta and Rome perished, what State can hope to last forever?' (3.11.1).

DEGENERATION AND COLLAPSE (3.10–11)

Whatever the underlying climactic and demographic factors, the proximate cause of the decline of the state is a consequence of a failing relationship between the government and the sovereign. The government – the prince – must and will end up acting not as the trustee of the sovereign but as its master. Rousseau tells us that this is a consequence of there being 'no other corporate will to resist the will of the Prince and so to balance it' (3.10.1). This is a remarkable claim in the light of what has gone before. In the first place, all of Rousseau's discussion of the appropriate ratios between sovereign, people and government was aimed at achieving the right balance between the need for the government to have sufficient force to keep the subjects in line and the need for the sovereign to control the government. The suggestion, then, was surely that the maintenance of the right ratios would be sufficient. Second, in the chapter on 'mixed governments' (3.7), Rousseau has explicitly made provision for division within the government to provide balancing corporate wills (3.7.4)! It is hard to see any great consistency here!

The degeneration of the state is, then, inevitable. It is a natural process. Rousseau uses two metaphors to describe this. First, he likens the state to the human body, fated to age from the moment of birth. Second, he compares the government to a watch: 'a Government never changes its form except where a worn-out mainspring leaves it too weak to preserve the form it has' (3.10.4). There are two main ways in which the government degenerates: contraction and the dissolution of the state.

Contraction seems to be an almost purely mechanical process which occurs as a smaller and smaller proportion of the citizenry participate in government. The suggestion here is that governments start off democratic and become progressively aristocratic and finally monarchical. Presumably (although Rousseau does not spell this out here) the growing alienation of the citizenry, due to increased numbers or luxury, results in the need for more repressive force and more efficient conduct of business. It is interesting that, once again, Rousseau describes this process in pejorative terms. If, as he said at 3.3.7, the different forms of government are each best in some circumstances and worst in others, why should the succession of one by the other, depending on change in those very circumstances, be described as 'degeneration'? Indeed, if it is typically *better* on grounds of the uprightness of the general will to be governed by an aristocracy rather than a democracy it is very peculiar for Rousseau to describe this as a change for the worse.

Contraction and dissolution do not, in any case, seem to be different ways of the government degenerating. Rather, contraction seems to be the necessary precursor of dissolution. Dissolution happens when the government either replaces the people as effective sovereign or when the various magistrates start to act on their own account rather than as a body. In the first of these two cases what we have is a state within a state, or rather a sovereign power enslaving most of the people. (It is hard to avoid the thought that Rousseau has the activity of the Genevan *Petit Conseil* in mind here.) In this instance he tells us that the usurpation constitutes a breach of the social pact and that the citizens are 'restored by right to their natural freedom' (3.10.6). As Maurice Halbwachs points out,[12] this highlights a difference between Locke and Rousseau. In Locke's theory, citizens maintain their natural rights both before and after the social contract and it is in the name of those rights that they may resist tyranny. For Rousseau, on the other hand, citizens who resist or protest against the abuse of government in the civil state do so in the name of the social pact; should that abuse reach the point where the social pact is no more, they return to a state of natural liberty where force, rather than law, mediates their relationship to others. For Locke then, natural rights are the fundamental ground of relations both within and without the civil state; for Rousseau a different kind of relationship exists among individuals once they are citizens together. Where the individual magistrates start to act on their own account, they are subverting the form of government established by the sovereign and acting against both sovereign and government.

An issue that naturally arises in such cases, for both Rousseau and Locke, is that of who is to judge when the founding agreement has been broken. On this question, Rousseau has little to say to us. Kant, by contrast, faced the problem squarely:

> And it would be an obvious contradiction if the constitution included a law . . . entitling the people to overthrow the existing constitution, from which all particular laws are derived, if the contract were violated. For there would then have to be a *publicly constituted* opposing power, hence a second head of state to protect the rights of the people against the first ruler, and then yet a third to decide which of the other two had right on his side.[13]

Kant's point here is that all talk of reserved rights against the sovereign power, whether such talk is couched in Lockean or in Rousseauian terms, is idle without a means to judge whether such rights have been violated. But who is to judge in such cases?

THE WELL-ORDERED STATE

What is the life of a well-ordered state like? That is the question which Rousseau seeks to address in the remainder of Book 3 where he articulates his vision of republican politics. This is a very different conception of the political from that found in, say, classical liberalism, libertarianism or in theories of democratic elitism. Politics is not a specialised task to be hived off to some team of elitists or technocrats and law is not simply there to provide a background of security and predictability against which private citizens can each pursue their private aims. Nor is political life conceived of as of purely instrumental value, a means to either individual or collective ends. Rather, the life of the citizen (and the collective lives of citizens together) is a form of life with its own distinct and intrinsic value. The achievement of this form of life is in the individual interest of each citizen, but this is not something that can be fully appreciated from outside that citizen identity: the goods of citizenship are fully attainable only by those who value citizenship intrinsically.

A striking feature of this collective life that Rousseau calls attention to is the constant activity, and indeed enthusiasm, of the citizens. It is not enough that the state be law-governed in a formal sense. Behind the letter of the law must always be the constant will of the citizens. 'It is not by Laws that the State subsists, it is by the legislative power' (3.11.4). In *Poland,* he provides for the constant re-examination and reaffirmation of the laws:

> . . . no law should ever be allowed to fall into disuse. Be it indifferent, be it bad, it should either be formally repealed or vigorously enforced. This maxim, which is fundamental, will require reviewing all ancient laws, repealing many of them, and attaching the most severe sanctions to those that are to be kept . . . Few laws, but well assimilated and above all well observed. All abuses that are not prohibited remain without consequence. But whoever, in a free State, invokes law, invokes that before which every Citizen trembles, and the King the first of all. In a word, tolerate anything rather than to wear out the spring of the laws; for once that spring is worn out, the State is lost without recourse.
>
> (G2: 223–4/OC3: 1002–3)

Since the legislative power is nothing but the people assembled as sovereign, this activity requires that such gatherings must be regular events.

The sovereign will assemble in two circumstances. First, there are 'extraordinary assemblies which may be required for unforseen circumstances', but there are also 'fixed and periodic assemblies which nothing can abolish or prorogue' (3.13.1). The magistrates have the power to call the people together for the extraordinary assemblies, and they have no power to prevent the regular ones. But outside of these two cases, the sovereign cannot, and may not, assemble 'because the order to assemble must itself emanate from law'. It is difficult to see why Rousseau is as restrictive as he is here.

Certainly his motive for preventing the citizens from assembling at other times has to be mainly pragmatic and to do with the stability of the state. For there is no reason in principle why the sovereign could not pass a law requiring the convening of the assembly if a certain proportion of the citizenry were to declare their wish that it be assembled.

Assembling the citizenry clearly places drastic limits on the size of the state. Rousseau brushes aside considerations of practicality in 3.12, perhaps forgetting that he himself had invoked these very considerations against democratic government earlier. Rousseau appeals (again) to the experience of the Greeks and Romans – and indeed the Macedonians and Franks – to counter the suggestion of impracticality. When he returns to the Greek experience at 3.15.9–10 it is to respond to the rather obvious suggestion that the Greeks were able to pursue a constantly active political life only at the expense of others: their slaves. To his credit, Rousseau does not duck this issue, but nor does he adequately resolve it. He tells us 'In some unfortunate circumstances one can preserve one's own freedom only at the expense of someone else's, and the Citizen can be perfectly free only if the slave is utterly enslaved' (3.15.10). But he does nothing to reassure us about the possibility of 'fortunate' circumstances in which this might not be so and relies instead on some rhetorical remarks about the self-enslavement of modern man.

The ideal state will be limited to a city and its surrounding countryside, ideally peopled fairly evenly and with the city very much subordinate to the countryside. Rousseau does make a gesture towards realism here – suggesting that larger states might have some system of moving assemblies of the people and peripatetic government (3.13.7), but it is clearly a concession that he makes reluctantly.

AGAINST REPRESENTATIVE SOVEREIGNTY (3.15)

Book 3 Chapter 15, 'Of Deputies or Representatives' is both one of the most important chapters of the *Social Contract*, and one of the most misunderstood. Many commentators have read Rousseau here as opposing representative *government*, but as we have seen, he objects rather to the representation of *sovereignty*. In 3.14, Rousseau actually makes clear that he sees the government as standing in a relation of representation to the people:

> The instant the People is legitimately assembled as Sovereign body, all jurisdiction of the Government ceases, the executive power is suspended, and the person of the last Citizen is as inviolable as that of the first Magistrate, *because where the Represented is, there is no longer a Representative*.
>
> (3.14.1, emphasis added)

But the government represents the people, acts on its behalf, not in making the laws, but in applying, interpreting and enforcing them. It may issue decrees on particular matters, but those must be within the legal and constitutional framework pre-established by the political community as a whole.

When Rousseau does discuss the representation of sovereignty, it is in a context where he is describing the moral corruption of the citizenry. Softened by luxury, citizens no longer have the public interest at the heart of their practical concerns. In two of their essential functions, defence of the state and formulation of the law, they are content to leave their duties to paid specialists: mercenary soldiers and professional politicians. Rousseau returns to the theme of his first *Discourse on the Sciences and Arts*:

> Sciences, Letters, and Arts . . . spread garlands of flowers over the iron chains with which they are laden, throttle in them the sentiment of that original freedom for which they seemed born, make them love their slavery, and fashion them into what is called civilized peoples.
>
> (G1: 6/OC3: 7)

Here again, 'It is the hustle and bustle of commerce and the arts, it is the avid interest in personal gain, it is softness and love of comforts that change personal services into money' (3.15.2). While pure self-sufficiency is beyond the reach of men in the civil state, the cultivation of expensive and sophisticated tastes and needs both softens citizens, making them less able and willing to bear hardship and sacrifice, and promotes an interdependence and mutual neediness that can fuel the reactive attitudes, including inflamed *amour propre*.

In a well-ordered society, there is little space for the fostering of a sense that one's own interests are sharply opposed to the collective ones: citizens, with a strong sense of common identity find it easy to see how what is decided in the assembly corresponds and fosters their own interests. By contrast, a corrupt society may well preserve the external form of free institutions but as citizens become more and more preoccupied with private concerns that they do not share with their fellows, the general will seems to them to have less practical importance for them. As attendance at the assembly falls due to public indifference, so does the cynicism of citizens increase as they see the sovereign assembly being manipulated for private objectives by those who remain: 'it is predictable that the general will will not prevail' (3.15.3).

The use of representatives to make law is, according to Rousseau, merely an expedient aiming to compensate for the moral corruption and political indifference of the citizens. But this is something that cannot be compensated for: it is a necessary condition for the emergence and maintenance of the general will that a sufficiently informed people deliberates and decides. Where the conditions to assure that this happens are lacking, no procedural fix will make up for it. In a reference back to 2.1, Rousseau tells us that sovereignty 'cannot be represented for the same reason that it cannot be alienated; it consists essentially in the general will' (3.15.5). In 2.1, Rousseau had sought to ground these claims about the inalienability and non-representability of the general will on the thought that, since particular wills always tend to partiality and the interests of particular individuals are opposed to one another, an accord between a particular will and the general will must be a contingent and temporary affair. To entrust lawmaking to a small group would be to invite them to pursue their private or corporate interests at the expense of the collective.

Despite Rousseau's hostility to the idea of representation in the *Social Contract*, it is noteworthy that he adopts a different attitude in other writings. In *Poland*, for example, he suggests that delegating the sovereign power has 'both bad and good aspects', but that the chief difficulty is that representatives are easily corrupted. He suggests that this can be countered, first, by having frequent elections (and concomitant frequent changes in representatives, perhaps assisted by term-limitations), thus raising the cost to the would-be corruptor. The second method is to tie the representatives to a fixed set of instructions (and he explicitly singles out for criticism the lack of restriction placed on English MPs during their seven-year terms) (G2: 201/OC3: 979).

The final three chapters of Book 3 offer further clarification of the sovereign–government relationship. In 3.16, Rousseau reaffirms the necessity for a body distinct from the sovereign to act in particular matters. The relationship between sovereign and government is not a contract between two parties, the government has no rights whatsoever vis-à-vis the sovereign, it simply has the task of acting on its behalf in particular matters. The sovereign's tasks are twofold: first it decides the form that government should take; second it entrusts the task of government to particular individuals. Rousseau anticipates the objection that this is a particular act and therefore not something that the sovereign can concern itself with: it is an application rather than an expression of the general will. He offers a simple solution: that the sovereign provisionally constitutes itself as a democratic government (a government of all the people) for the sole purpose of choosing the magistrates. Having once entrusted the government to a particular group of people, there is always the danger that they will usurp the power that properly belongs to the people: Rousseau's solution to this problem is to insist again on there being fixed periodic meetings of the sovereign assembly and that these meetings should always first consider (1) whether the present *form* of government should be retained and (2) whether the current group of magistrates should be retained or sacked.

HOW DEMOCRATIC ARE ROUSSEAU'S INSTITUTIONS?

Despite appearances, there remains some considerable uncertainty in Rousseau's account about the degree to which his institutions, taken as a whole, can be understood as democratic. Although, as we have seen, Rousseau's formal position is that the people are sovereign and the government is there to apply and enforce the law in particular cases, some critics have suggested that the real relationship between the two bodies might be one of elite domination of the people by the government.[14] There are certainly texts outside the *Social Contract* which suggest that the government would reserve legislative initiative to itself, and might also control the process whereby magistrates are selected: this giving rise to a picture of a self-selecting oligarchy with the people turning up in the assembly merely to rubber-stamp government proposals.[15] In the *Social Contract* itself, one passage in particular supports this view:

> I could offer quite a few reflections here on the simple right to vote in every act of sovereignty; a right of which nothing can deprive Citizens; and on the right of voicing opinions, proposing, dividing, discussing [motions], which the Government always takes great care to allow only to its own members . . .
>
> (4.1.7)

As Joshua Cohen has pointed out though,[16] this passage is somewhat ambiguous between description and prescription. Rousseau may be advocating such a restriction, or he may simply be telling us what the government will tend to do. Certainly it looks like an unsatisfactory basis for ascribing to Rousseau the position that the government should dominate, since so much of the discussion in Book 3 has centred on the *dangers* of this very possibility.

RECTITUDE, EFFICIENCY AND COMMONALITY

Book 3 of the *Social Contract* can be an unsatisfactory experience for the reader. The rather odd discussion of mathematical ratios and the disquisitions on the optimal size and climate of the good polity, have an undeniably archaic feel to them. Further, since most of what Rousseau deals with in the book concerns the 'maxims of politics', rather than 'principles of right', it can seem that we are considering matters of much lesser enduring importance than the material from the first two books. We are looking at the pragmatics of preserving a vibrant polity rather than at the principles of its just constitution.

Nevertheless, there are important lessons to be learned from the book, especially since it represents Rousseau's most extended discussion of the issues arising from one of his most important distinctions, that between the underlying principle of sovereignty, which must be retained by the people as a collective, and the task of putting the sovereign will into operation, which is normally the task of a specialised body, the government. What Rousseau has had to say on this matter represents a characteristic combination of the naïve and the insightful.

The naivety stems from the fact that his distinction between government and sovereign can seem over-sharp and, consequently, simple-minded. It is obvious to us today that the business of application and enforcement necessarily requires the interpretation of the law and so the suggestion that the government merely acts as the agent of the sovereign's antecedent will is somewhat unrealistic. The insightfulness lies in Rousseau's recognition of the importance of both culture and institutions and of their reciprocal effect on one another. The rule of the many is not merely a *procedural* matter. The simple fact that the people assemble, and that their votes are counted, is not sufficient to ensure that the state is a healthy and functioning one.

Rousseau's concern, throughout the book, has been to advocate institutions that get the balance right between the rectitude of the general will and the effectiveness of its implementation. Despite the mathematical analogies that he brings to bear on the problem, it is clear that he believes that there is no general formula that applies to all peoples at all times. After all, even those peoples who can achieve republican government – and many cannot – will vary significantly in virtue, population and resources. There is no escape from the dialectic between rectitude and effectiveness: if individuals are to adopt the right and virtuous attitude towards their institutions, they need a guarantee that the general will that they have willed together will actually restrain the conduct of their fellows. Without such a guarantee, the general will is sure to lapse into being a mere abstraction which the individual citizens do not see as being linked to the practical business of their lives. But the very body which provides citizens with such assurance is itself vulnerable to capture by self-interested individuals. The government can very easily become a tool of faction and can surreptitiously but effectively deprive the citizens of their sovereign power.

Particularly in 3.15, Rousseau stresses the importance of an active citizenry to counteract the possible capture of the state. But it is one thing to say that an active citizenry is necessary to the preservation of the state, it is another to bring and keep such a citizenry in being. That task was partly that of the lawgiver whom we considered in Chapter 7. Rousseau has further, related, ideas about building the common consciousness of citizens in Book 4 of the *Social Contract*, especially through the institution of a civil religion. This is our next topic.

NOTES

1 'But who is to guard the guards themselves?' Juvenal, *Satires*, no. 6, 1. 347.
2 Legislation rushed through to appease popular sentiment on a particular matter is almost always flawed and often unworkable. Recent examples in Britain include Kenneth Baker's notorious 'Dangerous Dogs Act'.
3 See, for example, Dworkin, *Law's Empire*, ch. 1.
4 Locke's discussion of these matters is at §§132–42 of the *Second Treatise of Government*. The key difference, of course, is that the people in Locke vest *lawmaking* power in the government. But Locke is clear that the form that government takes – its constitutional framework – is set by the people alone (see *Second Treatise*: §141).
5 The most extensive analysis of these passages is provided by Masters, *The Political Philosophy of Rousseau*, pp. 340–8. For Rousseau's mathematical language see Françon, 'Le Langage mathématique de Rousseau', pp. 85–8.
6 Rousseau refers to the 'corruption of the Lawgiver' as a danger in a democracy. It is clear from the context that he is not here writing of the lawgiver or great legislator of 2.7 but is, rather, making reference to the sovereign as a legislative body.
7 Fralin, *Rousseau and Representation*, p. 94.

8 Letter 2028 in CC, XII, p. 96.
9 See, especially, Frank Marini's neglected article, 'Popular Sovereignty but Representative Government, pp. 451–70.
10 See Hobbes, *Leviathan*, ch. 19.
11 Gildin, *Rousseau's Social Contract*, p. 122.
12 Halbwachs, *Jean-Jacques Rousseau: Du Contrat Social*, p. 323, n. 237.
13 Kant, 'On the Common Saying', p. 84.
14 See, especially, Fralin, *Rousseau and Representation*.
15 See the eighth *Letters from the Mountain*, especially at OC3: 346–7.
16 Cohen, 'Reflections on Rousseau', p. 291.

9

CIVIL RELIGION

(Book 4, Ch. 8)

Modern readers of the *Social Contract* typically encounter Book 4
Chapter 8 – 'Of Civil Religion' – with one of two reactions. The
first response is simply to ignore it; the second is to see the chapter
as further confirming evidence of illiberal and totalitarian elements
in Rousseau's thought. Neither of these opposing views is justified,
but they are united in contrasting sharply with the reactions of
Rousseau's own contemporaries. Along with the *Profession of Faith
of the Savoyard Vicar* from *Emile*, the chapter on civil religion was
seen as the most scandalous of Rousseau's writings. Those texts led
to the suppression of both books in Geneva, and the condemnation
of *Emile* by the Paris Parlement drove Rousseau into foreign exile.
The views that Rousseau expressed in them about Christianity and
its lack of contribution to the spirit of social solidarity outraged and
surprised his fellows even more than his prescription of the death
penalty for citizens who act as if they do not believe the tenets of
faith they have acknowledged has appalled hostile modern commentators. And yet this allegedly most illiberal of chapters contains some
striking concessions by Rousseau to modernity and pluralism and

anticipates in interesting ways some modern approaches to toleration, such as John Rawls's concept of an 'overlapping consensus' of 'reasonable comprehensive doctrines'.

Although the chapter does in some ways sit oddly alongside the rest of the *Social Contract* there are clear connections too. Rousseau plainly believes that social cohesion and patriotism, though they may be rationally justified, cannot be based simply on an appeal to the rational self-interest of citizens. The lawgiver had to attend to the psychology of patriotic identification, through song, dance, games and ritual, and Rousseau, fully aware of the power of religion, finally felt he had to address the issue of how religion might contribute to the working of a well-ordered society.

THE TEXT

The decision to include a discussion of the civil religion within the *Social Contract*, though so fateful for its initial reception, seems to have been one over which Rousseau hesitated. In December 1760, when Rousseau handed over the manuscript to his publisher, Rey, he did not include the chapter with the rest of the text and he seems to have added it as late as the autumn of 1761. That Rousseau saw the chapter as inessential to his main argument is also suggested by the fact that we do not find it summarised in *Emile*. On the other hand, Rousseau does seem to have entertained the basic ideas of the chapter over a very long period and we can find them spelt out in his *Letter to Voltaire* of 18 August 1756. The *Geneva Manuscript* also includes a draft, this time written on the verso of the chapter dealing with the lawgiver (and this is perhaps testimony to the crucial role played by religion in the lawgiver's work). An even earlier anticipation of the chapter's ideas is found in the *Discourse on Inequality*, where Rousseau tells us:

> . . . human Governments needed a much more solid base than reason alone, and how necessary it was for the public repose that the divine will intervene to endow the Sovereign authority with a sacred and inviolable character that might deprive subjects of the fatal Right to dispose of it. If Religion had performed only this good for men, it

would be enough for them all to have to cherish and adopt it, even with its abuses, since it still spares more blood than fanaticism causes to flow . . .

(G2: 181/OC3: 186)

Rousseau's conviction of the necessity of religion for social and political cohesion is thus a constant element in his writings and the task of the chapter is mainly to establish a positive content for that religion given the nature of men and the modern fact of religious pluralism.

THE HISTORY OF RELIGION (4.8.1–14)

The final version of the chapter naturally divides into three parts. In the first of these, Rousseau gives us an account of the history of religion and its relationship to state power from ancient times to the present. Second, he gives us a general classification of religions, settling on three religious types: the religion of man, the religion of the citizen, and the religion of the priests. Finally, in the final five paragraphs of the chapter, Rousseau sets out his positive programme, building on the work that he had already done in the *Letter to Voltaire*. There he tries to establish the role and limits of the sovereign in matters of religion and argues that social unity requires some shared (or at least overlapping) religious and moral commitments, and it is right that these be enforced in the form of the dogmas of civil religion.

The first forms of government, according to Rousseau were theocratic. He has the first peoples reasoning 'as had Caligula' (4.8.1). Here he refers us back to 1.2.6, 'Of the First Societies', where he tells us that, according to the Roman emperor, rulers were naturally a higher order of person than the ruled. But, the reader is surprised to discover, the first peoples 'reasoned correctly' in this respect, since it is very hard for people to accept that someone of the same kind as themselves has the right to rule. The necessity of theocratic government, argues Rousseau, naturally leads to polytheism, to the idea that there are (at least) as many gods as there are independent peoples. Thus, in early times, there is naturally a harmony between the demands of the state and law and the demands of religion. In those times there were no religious wars because each people recognised the limits of the legitimate domain of their own gods. Rousseau claims that this even applied to the Israelites, and cites an implicit recognition by the Jewish nation that other peoples had their gods and that these gods had legitimate authority within their own territory. All kinds of arrangements were, he claims, practically compatible with this attitude: so, for example, the Romans in extending their empire seem to have not only extended the domain of their own gods but also to have acquired large numbers of additional ones from their subject peoples.

This happy unity of politics and religion was destroyed, according to Rousseau, with the birth of Christianity. The idea of a parallel allegiance to a spiritual kingdom was quite contrary to the spirit of paganism and was seen by non-Christians merely as a hypocritical ruse by the Christians to enable them to bide their time until a new balance of power could enable them to take control (4.8.8). Rousseau seems to endorse this pagan view since he observes that once they were able to seize political power, 'the humble Christians changed their language, and before long this supposedly other-worldly kingdom was seen to become under a visible chief the most violent despotism in this world' (4.8.9). But even the triumph of Christianity did not solve the basic problem that it had created, namely that in recognising two kingdoms, two domains of competence – the religious and the secular – sovereignty and authority had been fatally divided and 'no one has ever succeeded in settling the question of which of the two, the master or the priest, one is obliged to obey' (4.8.10). Although Rousseau seems to favour a strictly theological explanation for this division into two competing powers, this is not entirely borne out by what he says about Islam. As Rousseau recognises, Islam does not distinguish between secular and religious authority (at least in the ideal case) but he sees this division being imposed upon them due to the conquest of Muslims by 'barbarians' as a consequence of luxury setting in and their manners being softened (4.8.11). Islam, especially the Shi'ite variety, is very much in the same position as Christianity.

Rousseau credits Hobbes, above all, with understanding that this division of authority was fatal to a well-ordered society. Hobbes 'dared to propose reuniting the two heads of the eagle' (4.8.13). Indeed, the reader who consults Hobbes's writings will see that he is everywhere concerned with the damaging consequences to political order of the pretension of religion to independent authority. In *Leviathan*, and elsewhere, Hobbes repeatedly attacks the idea that sovereignty might be divided between temporal and spiritual concerns:

> . . . where one is Soveraign, another Supreme; where one can make Lawes, and another make Canons, there must needs be two Commonwealths, of one & the same Subjects; which is a Kingdome divided in it selfe, and cannot stand.
>
> (*Leviathan*, ch. 29, p. 227)

In *De Cive*, Hobbes makes the point that the death penalty is as nothing compared to the fear of eternal damnation:

> For no man can serve two masters; nor is he less, but rather more a master whom we believe we are to obey for fear of temporal damnation, than he whom we obey for fear of temporal death. It follows therefore that this one, whether man or court, to whom the city hath committed the supreme power, have also this right; that he both judge what opinions and doctrines are enemies unto peace, and also that he forbid them to be taught.
>
> (*De Cive*, 6, 11)

Rousseau actually goes beyond Hobbes at this point, since he seems to suggest that Hobbes's 'solution' will never work: that the 'domineering spirit' of Christianity can never really be subordinated to secular authority. As we shall see, this seems contrary to the spirit of civil religion as he outlines it later in the chapter.

TYPES OF RELIGION IN RELATION TO THE STATE (4.8.15–30)

Rousseau's apparent hostility to Christianity intensifies when he ventures a threefold classification of religious types as they relate to the state: the religion of man, the religion of the citizens and the religion of the priests. The third of these, the religion of the priests, which explictly sets up a religious body with the authority to command alongside the state, is manifestly defective on the Hobbesian grounds just discussed: it gives subjects two masters and contradictory duties. The classic form of this seems to be Roman Catholicism, but Rousseau mentions Buddhism and Shintoism for good measure. But it is the first two forms – the religion of man and the religion of the citizen – that command Rousseau's attention.

The 'religion of the citizen' corresponds to the first of the historical forms Rousseau has already examined. The gods are particular to nations and the 'rights and duties of man' only extend as far as the borders of the state (4.8.15). This form of religion is highly conducive to political stability and social solidarity: love of God and love of the laws are combined within a single institution. But even though some of the purely political effects of this form are good, they are not sufficient to outweigh its manifest defects. The religion of the citizen is to be rejected because it is *false* and thus induces superstitious beliefs in the citizenry. Rousseau's attitude to religion, even in relation to the state, is not, therefore a purely pragmatic one. He cares not just about what a religion can achieve politically but also whether its articles of faith are rationally defensible. The second major fault with the religion of the citizen is that it makes its believers antagonistic to surrounding peoples. If each people believes itself to be chosen and also believes that it has no duties towards its neighbours, peoples will be drawn into vicious wars with one another. So, though this form of religion is good for the internal cohesion of a people, it cannot be commended as being congenial to their long-term survival.

The 'religion of man' which Rousseau moves onto next, has somewhat the opposite faults: it is good for peace between peoples (or would be if they all espoused it) but contributes nothing to their internal solidarity. This 'religion of man', is basically a non-doctrinaire Christianity. It enjoins men to universal peace and brotherhood. Rousseau's principal political objections to such a religion are twofold. First, he argues – consistently with his critique of the idea of a 'general will of the human race' from ch. 2 of the *Geneva Manuscript* – that although adherence to a universal morality may be admirable, given 'men as they are' there is insufficient motive for compliance with such a morality and those that are motivated to comply simply end by delivering themselves into the hands of the unjust and rapacious. Good Christians, then, are easy prey for a 'Cromwell' or a 'Cataline' (4.8.26). Second, Rousseau asserts that Christians are indifferent to the success or failure of worldly institutions: their attention is on the next world and not on this one. These are opinions that Rousseau takes more or less ready-made from Machiavelli: in the *Discourses* (II.2), Machiavelli puts matters thus:

> Our religion . . . places the supreme happiness in humility, lowliness, and a contempt for worldly objects, whilst the other, on the contrary, places the supreme good in grandeur of the soul, strength of body, and all such other qualities as render men formidable; and if our religion claims of us fortitude of soul, it is more to enable us to suffer that to achieve great deeds.
>
> These principles seem to have made men feeble, and caused them to become an easy prey to evil-minded men, who can control them more securely, seeing that the great body of men, for the sake of gaining Paradise, are more disposed to endure injuries than to avenge them.

Christians, then, because of this indifference to the affairs of this world and their attitudes of humility and resignation, cannot function as good citizens of a republic 'taking men as they are, and the laws as they can be' (1.0.1). This belief of Rousseau's attracted the most sustained hostility, and, following the condemnation of the *Social Contract* he had to engage in a series of defences and clarifications of his views in correspondence and in the *Letters from the Mountain*. In his letter to Usteri of 18 July 1763, for example, he expresses his admiration for pure Christianity and yet maintains his position essentially unchanged. Rousseau there argues that his topic is politics and the organisation of social life. Universal pure Christianity would be fine, and indeed would sustain a regime of universal brotherhood. But the very need for political association arises from the fact that this condition of spontaneous compliance with universal morality does not obtain. The Christians whom we find among us are not saints, they are men, and subject to the passions of men. Men need political institutions. Those institutions, in turn, need affective support from citizens and they cannot get enough of this from the 'religion of man'.

ROUSSEAU'S POSITIVE PROGRAMME (4.8.31–5)

So, given the shortcomings of both the religion of the citizen and the religion of man, Rousseau needs to spell out what the religious requirements of the just society are. His comments are, unfortunately, somewhat brief and leave many issues hanging in the air. He plainly builds on his earlier thoughts, expressed in his *Letter to Voltaire* of 1756. In that work he distinguishes between three aspects of religion: private belief, official doctrine, and outward behaviour. The first of these is, he argues, simply outside of the domain of possible political authority: even if the sovereign wished to control what citizens believe he cannot have access to their inner thoughts. Even if he could, since belief is outside voluntary control and citizens therefore cannot just will what to believe, the attempt to control such matters is vain and beyond human power (G2: 244/OC4: 1072). But Rousseau also argues that simply to shift the focus of political concern to outward behaviour would be a mistake: 'Fanatics change their language as their fortune changes, and when they are not the strongest, they preach nothing but patience and gentleness'. Any doctrine that officially condemns those who do not subscribe to it as immoral is to be rejected and is not to be tolerated, including the doctrine of 'intolerant nonbelievers who wanted to force the people to believe nothing'. In the *Letter*, then, Rousseau suggests that there should be a civil profession of faith which should consist of 'those social maxims everyone would be bound to acknowledge' and a list of the fanatical maxims that have to be rejected 'not as impious, but as seditious'. Citizens are free to adopt any religion that is in conformity with this code or even to adopt the code itself as their religion (G2: 245/OC4: 1073).

One obvious difficulty with the code as Rousseau has formulated it in the *Letter* is that it seems to be self-contradictory. It bans doctrines just in case they condemn as immoral anyone who fails to conform with them: but it looks as if the civil religion itself does this. A little reconstruction can save Rousseau from the appearance of incoherence. Intolerant doctrines reject other codes of belief on the ground that they are *false* (they also assert that the adherents of those false beliefs are bad, or damned, people). But the civil religion makes no assertion about the truth or falsity of bodies of doctrine: it simply assesses their conformity with the possibility of a well-ordered society. People who claim that only the adherents of their own sect are saved will be meddlesome in the affairs of others – indeed they have a duty to meddle – as such they are not conducive to a united citizenry.

In the *Social Contract*, Rousseau sketches a civil profession of faith in a similar manner: the sovereign has 'no competence in the other world' (4.8.31) and so has no right to force some beliefs rather than others on the citizens. But the sovereign does have competence in this world, and insofar at it is not possible to be a good citizen without believing (or appearing to believe) in certain principles, it is permissible and even mandatory for the sovereign to insist that all citizens adhere to those principles. What, according to Rousseau are these dogmas? They are five: first, that benevolent deity exists; second, that there will be life after death; third, that the just will be rewarded and the wicked punished; fourth, that the social contract and the laws are sacred; and, finally, fifth, that sectarian intolerance is prohibited (4.8.33).

Rousseau's insistence on the first three articles of the civil religion may appal modern readers. But it is important to note that he was very much in accord with what his contemporaries thought. Indeed, it was a commonplace of seventeenth- and eighteenth-century thought that atheists, believing that they did not face divine punishment, could not be trusted to act morally. So, for example, John

Locke, in his *Letter Concerning Toleration*, insisted on including atheists among those who are not to be tolerated: 'Promises, covenants, and oaths, which are the bonds of human society, can have no hold upon an atheist. The taking away of God, though but even in thought, dissolves all.'[1]

Rousseau, then, in demanding that citizens affirm belief in a God is simply echoing conventional opinion. More worrying, perhaps, is Rousseau's account of the consequences of non-adherence. In the first instance, those who do not sign up for the civil creed are to be banished from the state (4.8.32); but if someone remains and 'behaves as if he did not believe them, let him be punished with death' (4.8.32). What, if anything, can be said to make Rousseau's thoughts here more palatable?

The first thing we should note is that Rousseau's concern here is always with establishing the conditions of good social order. The sovereign people establish the articles of the civil profession of faith 'not precisely as dogmas of Religion, but as sentiments of sociability, without which it is impossible to be either a good Citizen or a loyal subject' (4.8.32). Although Rousseau himself suggests the particular articles he lists, it would be open to the sovereign people to approve other ones. As Rousseau reminds us, the authority of the sovereign over the subjects does not 'exceed the bounds of public utility' (4.8.31), so should Rousseau's empirical belief that the first three articles are necessary conditions of sociability prove false, his argument would not justify their inclusion. Rousseau is not, then, trying to foist any particular sectarian dogmas on society; he is simply trying to give the social bond enough strength to persist over time. Those who are banished from the state because they cannot accept the articles are cast out of the society 'not as impious but as unsociable' (4.8.32). This thought also lies behind a passage from his *Letter to De Beaumont* which is at least *in tension* with what he had said in the *Letter to Voltaire* about the limits of the sovereign's competence:

> On what grounds does a man have the right to inspect the beliefs of another, and why does the state have the right to inspect the beliefs of its citizens? It is because we assume that the beliefs of men deter-

mine their morals, and that their conduct in this life depends on the ideas they have concerning the life to come. When this is not so, what does it matter what they believe or pretend to believe? The appearance of religion only serves to exempt them from having one.

In society each person has the right to inform himself whether or not another person believes himself to be obliged to be just, and the Sovereign has the right to examine the grounds on which each person affirms this obligation.

(OC4: 973)

His thought here seems to be that citizens need to be mutually assured that one another will be reliable co-operators, will not cheat or break their agreements. The civil religion, so long as it is not hypocritically affirmed can give citizens a confidence in dealing with one another, a confidence that will underpin their feelings of common identity and solidarity.

What, then, of his prescription of the death penalty for those who affirm the articles but make it clear from their conduct that they do not believe them? Rousseau nowhere makes the least attempt to spell out for us what sort of behaviour would count as signifying that a person did not believe in the articles. There is little more to be said on this matter beyond acknowledging the extremely unsatisfactory nature of Rousseau's brief and bloodthirsty comments and noting that in another context, Rousseau is far less keen on the idea of imposing the death penalty for religious nonconformity. In *Julie* he writes: 'If I were a judge, and the law prescribed the death penalty against atheists, I would begin by having burned for atheism anyone who came to turn in someone else'.[2] It has to be something of an open question which of these declarations represents his considered view on the subject. Taking his work as a whole, however, there is little evidence that he would favour such extreme sanction for *delit d'opinion*: and this is perhaps just as well in someone brought up as a Calvinist, converted to Catholicism, reconverted and then condemned by all for his strange religious heterodoxy.

A focus on Rousseau's mention of the death penalty and on the fact that he seems to prescribe an official religion, rather deflects attention from the interestingly tolerant and liberal aspects of the chapter. In fact, Rousseau is very far from any insistence that there be a dogmatic national ideology. Rather, he is aware of the fact that religious disagreement is a persistent and ineliminable feature of modern life: 'there no longer is and no longer can be an exclusive national religion' (4.8.35). The articles of the civil profession of faith are the minimum necessary to ensure social cohesion and are framed in such a way that believers from a wide range of confessional backgrounds can affirm them. They 'ought to be simple, few in number, state with precision, without explanations or commentary' (4.8.33). The elements of the civil religion can certainly be affirmed from within the main Christian traditions, as well as by Jews, Muslims and deists.

Rousseau insists on one 'negative dogma': he rejects intolerance. This dogma does not simply involve the state avoiding intolerance of different religions, it involves the proscription of religions which cannot live at peace with their rivals. '[W]hoever dares to say, *no Salvation outside the Church*, has to be driven out of the State' (4.8.35). Theological intolerance, he tells us, is bound to have effects in society and to disrupt civic unity. For example, if priests are given the right to decide what is to count as a valid marriage they will use this to promote the doctrine of their sect.

CONCLUSION

The chapter on civil religion may contain oddities and excesses that concern modern liberals. But Rousseau was trying to face squarely an issue which many would pretend is not there: namely, how can we build an affective unity of citizens, that is both consistent with a degree of pluralism and tolerance and which can sustain the liberties citizens enjoy together. In the lengthy footnote from *Emile* where he discusses fanaticism (E4: 312n/OC4: 632–3), Rousseau had doubted whether mere considerations of rational self-interest would be sufficient to unite men in a flourishing state. The 'reasoning and philosophic spirit', he conjectured would tend to dissociate people from one another, a process which would no doubt be exacerbated by their tendency to put their reasoning at the service of selfishness and *amour propre*. The experience of communes and other utopian communities down the years would tend to bear out Rousseau's worries, those based around shared religious beliefs have survived much better than those organised according to purely secular ideals.[3] Yet he recognised that the time had passed when any thickly specified set of religious beliefs could be held in common by co-citizens: social unity required at least that Calvinists and Catholics could coexist together in mutual respect. We might not agree with the details of Rousseau's civil religion, but he may well be right that successful citizenship needs not just self-interest and abstract principle, but also things like shared symbolism, tradition, music and ritual. The perfected institutions that reshape the independent man of the *Geneva Manuscript* do not achieve his reshaping simply, or even mainly, by giving him good arguments.

NOTES

1 Locke, *A Letter Concerning Toleration*, p. 47.
2 *Julie or the New Heloise*, p. 482/OC2: 589n.
3 See Taylor, *Community, Anarchy and Liberty*, p. 163.

10

THE *SOCIAL CONTRACT* IN RETROSPECT

Rousseau set out his aim in the *Social Contract* clearly enough. It was to find a state that managed to combine the authority necessary to co-ordinate the private activity of its constituent members without their giving up the right of directing themselves. Rousseauian citizens were to remain, 'as free as before' (1.6.4). In the near quarter of a millennium since Rousseau was writing, the claim that the ideal state described and advocated there is a locus of individual freedom has come under sustained attack. Many critics have charged that the freedom allegedly enjoyed by the citizens there is a fraud or a sham, and that the real picture generated by Rousseau is one of totalitarianism or despotism. The volume of these criticisms and the fact that they have been sustained over two centuries by writers who otherwise differ sharply in their philosophical and political outlooks, mean that we should take them seriously. Whether they are ultimately well founded, is, of course, an issue that depends on the examination and interpretation of the detail of Rousseau's texts. In fact, there are a cluster of questions and issues that surround the post-Rousseauian debate, some of which are textual, others of which are political, historical and, indeed, ideological in nature. This final chapter aims to survey some of this material.

One odd feature of the afterlife of the general will is worth remarking on. The concept has been influential in both political thought and in philosophical method, but Rousseau's critics and successors in these two areas have typically attacked the idea from opposite directions. So, in the field of political thought and argument, hostile commentators have seen in the general will something abstract and ideal to be contrasted with the actual wants, desires and beliefs of the citizenry. The spirit of Robespierre or of the vanguard party of Lenin is often invoked as an awful warning of the consequences of such an idealising move. In philosophy, by contrast, where the concern has been to use concepts derivative of the general will as tools or methods of right reason, Rousseau's general will is often seen as insufficiently idealised: so, for example, Kant, Hegel and Rawls have, in their various ways each sought to make use of some notion derivative of the general will, but one purified of the imperfections of real people.

POLITICAL HOSTILITY

Much of the twentieth-century hostility towards Rousseau was plainly ideological and dictated by the contingencies of politics. The socialist movement was, perhaps, the biggest secular mass movement in the history of the world. It aimed to reshape society so as to overcome both class division and the alienation of the market. In the west, it threatened or promised to take power through elections thanks to the numerical preponderance of the industrial working class. In eastern Europe, parties claiming socialist inspiration took power as a result first of revolution in Russia and, subsequently, because of the success of the Red Army in defeating Nazi Germany. Liberal scholars, believing this movement to threaten both individual liberty and private property, naturally engaged in sharp philosophical and ideological critique, not just of Marxism, but also of its intellectual antecedents. Jean-Jacques Rousseau featured among those seen to have inspired the socialist tradition.

This was hardly an unreasonable association to make. Rousseau was a critic, *avant la lettre*, of capitalist society. Although, as we have seen, Rousseau sometimes describes himself as having the same principles as John Locke, he is, in fact, deeply critical of the idea of a market society based on relations between individual owners of property. In the *Discourse on Inequality* he had attacked the notion that formal equality before the law and the guarantee of security of property and the person would protect people from domination by others. Rather, he was keenly sensitive – indeed sometimes oversensitive – to the ways in which both market and hierarchical relationships could conceal oppression and exploita-tion behind a veneer of voluntary agreement. Individuals, be they masters or servants, could come to depend on others both for their material well-being and, more importantly for Rousseau, for their own good opinion of themselves. The play of pretence and dissimulation in such settings was, for him, deeply subversive of the possibility of leading a good, and truly human, life.

At the centre of the case against Rousseau has been a cluster of alleged commitments in his political philosophy. First, critics have focused on his distinction between the general will and the will of all in Book 2 Chapter 3 of the *Social Contract* to suggest that, far from his state being genuinely democratic, the 'real' will of the citizens might be invoked against their actual decision. Second, the 'total alienation' involved in the social pact has seemed to leave the citizen no recourse against an all-powerful sovereign. Third, the indivisibility of the sovereign power has seemed to rule out any system of checks and balances or the independent judiciary charac-teristic of liberal democracies. Also, the democratic mechanisms invoked by Rousseau seem to leave the citizenry at the mercy of an elite government, since Rousseau appears to wish to rule out political parties and other forms of citizen self-organisation. Finally, there is the issue of the manipulation of the will: the manipulation of the citizens by the lawgiver, its parallels to the activity of the tutor in *Emile*, Rousseau's remarks on 'denaturing' in *Emile* and the fostering of a state religion all have a sinister feel to them, particularly in the light of subsequent events.

'TOTALITARIANISM' AND THE GENERAL WILL

The thought that there is a totalitarian strand in Rousseau's thought may take its inspiration from the idea that the general will somehow incarnates the 'real' will of the citizens in a way that comes apart from the idea they themselves have of what they want. This thought can have two sources, which we should consider independently of one another. The first, individualist, version of this concern derives from Rousseau's insistence that citizens will the general will even when they are in a minority. The collective version of this concern centres on the possible separation of the general will from the actual decision of the people. These are clearly very different issues and they should be looked at in turn.

The individualist version of this worry is, at one level, just a statement with reference to Rousseau, of a common thought about democratic government and individual rights. If we allow the law to be set by the people, with no checks and balances, then we appear to open the possibility of the 'tyranny of the majority'. If there are majorities and minorities, then some people will be compelled to comply with laws that they did not favour and we can raise the question of why they are obliged to do so. Rousseau is certainly insufficiently alive to this problem. When he tells us, for example, that 'The Sovereign, by the mere fact that it is, is always everything it ought to be' (1.7.5), blithely asserting that since the people constitute the sovereign it could have no interests contrary to theirs, he displays a shocking lack of imagination. We can, after all, all too easily conceive of majorities of individuals who, acting for the best of altruistic motives, act to limit the freedom of their fellows 'in their own best interests'.

While this problem of possible popular tyranny arises quite generally for theories of democracy it is exacerbated in the *Social Contract* by the fact that Rousseau's conception of sovereignty is as unlimited as that of Hobbes. The sovereign people may be constrained to command in the form of general and universal laws, but there is no restriction of principle on what it may command in that form. There is no protected domain of individual action where the sovereign may not intervene. Where Rousseau seems to endorse the idea of such a protected private sphere, he immediately qualifies that endorsement by leaving the sovereign as judge of its legitimate extent.

These practical threats to individual freedom from democratic decision-making and unlimited sovereignty are further deepened in the eyes of liberal readers by Rousseau's apparent attempts to theorise away the whole issue of individual freedom. For example, he insists that the individual who is in the minority gets what he *really* wants when the majority prevails, and he tells us that people who are made to conform with the laws of the state are 'forced to be free'. So not only do we have a limitation of freedom by democracy – some version of which liberals will certainly accept the inevitability of – but also the seemingly outrageous denial that this is a restriction of freedom at all, indeed the assertion that such is freedom's realisation!

We can, however, put together the elements of a Rousseauian response to these concerns. Social life together inevitably involves a restriction on our freedom and, given the historical development of the human race we have no choice but to live together in society. Both our material well-being and our sense of who we are and what we are worth is, for better or worse, inevitably bound up with the lives we share with others. An assessment of how far and in which ways a set of political institutions restricts our freedom therefore inevitably raises the question: compared to what? A Hobbesian state of nature where relations among individuals are mediated by force rather than law is clearly, Rousseau would argue, defective from the point of view of freedom compared to a society governed by a general will since the freedom people enjoy there is of no value to them. A Lockean state, though guaranteeing a formal equality before the law, allows substantial inequalities of power and property which entrench relations of both material and psychological dependence and hence renders individuals subject to the will of particular others. The state Rousseau advocates in the *Social Contract* restricts freedom in two ways. First, the sovereign people assigns rights to individuals which have the effect of restricting the freedom of other individuals (so, the right I have over my person and property restricts your freedom to make use of my person and property).

Second, the people retains the capacity to intervene in individuals' deployment of their rights to block the emergence of Lockean-style inequalities. But in each of these two cases, freedom is restricted for the sake of freedom. The individual who is 'forced to be free' is constrained to guarantee the conditions under which he and others can both coexist and be free consistent with that coexistence; the individual who is in a minority might not get what they immediately want, but they do get what they most deeply want, namely continuing social life with others on reasonable terms.

How plausible is this Rousseauian response? Negatively, there is still much to worry about concerning the operation of the specific institutions Rousseau advocates. The nosy and intrusive preferences of one's fellow citizens may still get free reign in such a constitution and may place restrictions on individual freedom that are not justified for the sake of freedom itself. But positively, we can say that Rousseau attends to the need to maintain the conditions under which individuals can freely coexist with other individuals. Notably, in allowing that disparities of wealth and income may undermine both the freedom individuals enjoy and the integrity of their equal citizenship, Rousseau at least points the way for others to develop his insights. Such has been the programme, in various ways of socialist, social-democratic, egalitarian liberal and civic republican thinkers since Rousseau's own day.[1]

The collective version of the concern that the general will prioritises the 'real will' of citizens above what they actually want is, I believe, less well supported by the text of the *Social Contract* than the individualist version is. The proximate source of this worry is, of course, Rousseau's distinction between the general will and the 'will of all' in Book 2, Chapter 3. But, as I have endeavoured to argue, this is best understood not as articulating the thought that some abstract general will other than what the citizens have voted ought to be enforced. Rather, Rousseau's concern there is the entirely reasonable one of sketching how democratic decision-making can misfire if it is exercised in conditions of ignorance, passion and, particularly, when subject to the distorting pressures of power and inequality. But although there is little licence in Rousseau for separating the general will off from what the people actually decide (at least under favourable conditions) the subsequent history of the idea has indulged just such a separation on both the political and philosophical planes, and this has been read back into Rousseau.

As a matter of history and practice, the sundering of the general will from the decision of the people is a fruit of the French Revolution. Rousseau's own comments on French society are nearly always uncomplimentary, indeed he argued that the French language was unsuitable as the language of a free people. France was a large society, the most populous state in Europe at the time, and one, moreover, riven by sharp inequalities of wealth and dramatic differences in status. In fact, it is hard to imagine a contemporary society further away from the ideal of small size, absence of luxury, rough equality of fortune and commonality of manners that Rousseau thought were background preconditions for a just society. In particular, the core idea of Rousseauian sovereignty, that the general will could not be alienated or represented but that the people themselves should be directly sovereign, was impossible to implement on the scale of French society. This did not mean, of course, that those who participated in, and led, the revolution were uninfluenced by Rousseau's ideas, but the conception of representative sovereignty that was promoted by the Abbé de Sièyes was diametrically opposed to Rousseau's own view. Robespierre's contention that the Committee of Public Safety constituted the general will was doubly anti-Rousseauian: not only does it breach Rousseau's strictures against the representation of sovereignty but it also nullifies Rousseau's principled distinction between the sovereign and the government, since the Committee was concerned with the application and enforcement of the law in particular cases.[2]

Subsequent to the revolution, all manner of movements and politicians have laid claim to the 'will of the people' in one form or another, and political parties have, of course, claimed to incarnate the will of the proletariat. At some times these claims have been backed up with some connection to what the putatively represented actually thought about the issue, at others their empirical beliefs about the matter have been considered irrelevant. Needless to say, none of these claims has much to do with Rousseau or the general will.

TOTAL ALIENATION

Another aspect of the *Social Contract* that has consistently inspired alarm among liberals and libertarians has been Rousseau's insistence that at the moment of the social pact there is a 'total alienation of each associate with all of his rights to the whole community' (1.6.6). We can contrast this picture of total alienation with a typically Lockean view of the relationship between the individual and the state. In the American Declaration of Independence, for example, we find Jefferson writing that men 'are endowed by their Creator with certain inalienable Rights'. Jefferson uses the standpoint of natural rights to voice a critique of the abuse of power. But so long as the sovereign community retains its nature as such, so long, at least as 'the characteristics of the general will are in still in the majority' (4.2.8), it seems that there is no such critical perspective available to Rousseau's citizens. Since Rousseau offers no clear criteria to judge whether the body that has the formal characteristics of a sovereign assembly actually is one, there is clearly an acute difficulty. Suppose an assembly, open to all the citizens, passes a law which some individuals experience as oppressive. Since they retain no rights against the sovereign, if the assembly is sovereign, then they have no cause for complaint or resistance. But perhaps they should take the passing of an apparently oppressive law as a sign that the assembly is no longer what it claims to be? Perhaps a faction has become dominant? There is a worrying suspicion of undecidability here.

Despite superficial appearances, though, Lockean right-holders are really no better off than Rousseauian citizens. Faced with an alleged abuse of power by a Lockean state, they may well protest and complain. But who is competent to judge whether such an abuse has taken place? Clearly, neither an outcome where each individual is authoritative on this matter, nor one where the state is, is going to be satisfactory. In practice, the Lockean question of whether the preassociational rights of the individual have been violated is as hard to answer as the Rousseauian question of whether the body that purports to possess the characteristics of sovereignty continues to have them.

CONSTITUTIONALISM AND ELITE DOMINATION?

In reality, states as human associations, whatever attitude they take theoretically to the rights of the individual, need institutional and constitutional devices to protect individuals. Here, perhaps, Rousseau's polity may seem to fall short. His account of the functioning of a just state may have inspired democrats down the years, but serious questions have been raised about how democratic his vision of the well-ordered society actually was. One of his chief theoretical innovations was his distinction between government and sovereign and he repeatedly insists upon the supremacy of the latter over the former. The sovereign people make the laws in the form of general and universal regulations and the government applies and enforces those laws – that is the official picture. But when we examine the relationship between the two bodies more closely, it may appear that the government – the magistrates – would, in fact, dominate the people. To be sure, Rousseau insists on there being periodic assemblies, which the magistrates have no right to cancel and where the question of their continued tenure of office must be put, but outside of these fixed dates, the people have no right to convene themselves as sovereign in order to remove or sanction the government. In the application of the general principles that the citizens have decided upon, it looks as if the magistrates have the discretion to interpret them as they choose: there is certainly no independent judicial body to which aggrieved citizens could appeal against an abuse of power. And the initiative in the legislature looks to be firmly in the hands of the government, to the point where Rousseau at one instance seems to say that only magistrates have the right of 'voicing opinions, proposing, dividing, discussing [motions]' (4.1.7) although, to be fair, as we have seen, it is unclear whether Rousseau's comments are prescriptive or simply mean to characterise the probable practice of, possibly abusive, governments. Then there is the ban on factions in the assembly, which Rousseau proposes at 2.3.4, ostensibly to permit the general will to emerge without the distorting influence of wealth and power but which would predictably have the effect of leaving only one group regularly disposing of political organisation: again, the magistrates.

Rousseau's ban of the representation of sovereignty may also have the paradoxical effect of strengthening the hand of the government vis-à-vis the people. It is a staple of constitutional and democratic theory from Burke to Weber that a parliament composed of educated, committed and aware legislators is necessary to hold executives to account. Through mechanisms such as parliamentary or congressional committees, skilled politicians (often trained as lawyers) can ask tough questions of ministers and civil servants. Rousseau wants to take 'men as they are', but arguably, for the citizenry to keep the government in check would require a level of citizen commitment that seems unrealistic to us. Of course, if the just state is to be composed of peasants sitting under trees and debating their affairs in common (4.1.1) this problem may be easily surmounted. But the cost, in terms of relevance to our concerns and problems is probably too high: Rousseau's 'realistic utopianism' will seem all too utopian.

THE LAWGIVER, CIVIL RELIGION, DENATURING AND ENGULFMENT

Critics have also, understandably, worried about the mysterious figure of the lawgiver or legislator. Again, although Rousseau has an official doctrine of popular sovereignty, he appears to allow for the manipulation of the popular will by a person not subject to any democratic control. Moreover, this person does not operate by advancing arguments, by attempting to appeal to the reason of citizens, but rather manipulates their affections by means of rhetoric, religion and ceremony. Understandably, this has struck many critics as sinister. When we add into the mix Rousseau's penchant for this type of character in his other writings – notably the tutor in *Emile* and Wolmar in *Julie* – and look at his comments in *Emile* about how good social institutions would strip man of his nature and give him a purely artificial character and then proceed to consider the chapter on civil religion, the prospect of Rousseau-as-liberal looks remote.

There is nothing to be said at this point fully to answer the critic who is determined to read the *Social Contract* by the light of some passages from *Emile* and *Julie*. What can be argued is that much of the *Social Contract* points in other directions, that he explicitly tells us that the citizen retains much of his pre-citizen nature (2.4.2), and that it is to Rousseau's credit that he explicitly faces the issue of whether a viable state can be woven from the cloth of reason, morality and self-interest without the help of symbolism, ritual and passion. Rousseau's image of the good society is heavily influenced by ancient models – such as Rome and Sparta – but though such influence finds expression in some of his 'totalitarian' formulations, it does not accurately sum up his project for a just society taking 'men as they could be'.

THE PHILOSOPHICAL AFTERLIFE OF THE GENERAL WILL

If, in politics, Rousseau has been criticised for allegedly divorcing the general will from the actual choices of the citizens, in philosophy he has been taken to task for not doing so. The idea of the general will has, there, been developed as a tool of abstract reasoning and argument. Kant, for example, was plainly influenced in his moral theory by Rousseau (though in a direction that paradoxically moves him closer to Diderot's view as criticised by Rousseau at Chapter 2 of the *Geneva Manuscript*). Famously, Kant proclaimed Rousseau to be the 'Newton of the moral sciences' and we can see the shadow of the *Social Contract* in the idea in the *Groundwork of the Metaphysic of Morals* that the moral agents should consider themselves as legislating for a kingdom of ends. When Kant moves from strictly moral to political philosophy we also encounter the social contract and the general will, but again, not as implementable in the life of a people but as 'an idea of reason' against which to test the legitimacy of legislation. Whereas, for Rousseau, the legitimacy of a law depended on its actually resulting from the people's decision, for Kant it is the mere hypothetical possibility of such a decision that is crucial: a law is to be considered legitimate unless the people could not have given their assent to it. While Kant is willing to give us examples of laws that could not pass such a test – for example, a law to institute a hereditary ruling class – it is clearly a very weak constraint on legitimacy.

Kant's successor in the pantheon of German idealism, Hegel, also drew on Rousseau in formulating the idea that the state ought to be governed according to a universal will. But even more than with Kant, the Hegelian will is far removed from what the people choose. In fact, Hegel seeks *in principle* to reject the connection with the wants and desires of the citizens. In the *Encyclopaedia Logic*, Hegel explicitly rebukes Rousseau for his alleged confusions:

> The distinction between ... what is merely in common, and what is truly universal, is strikingly expressed by Rousseau in his famous *Contrat social*, when he says that the laws of a state must spring from the universal will (volonté générale), but need not on that account be the will of all (*volonté de tous*). Rousseau would have made a sounder contribution towards a theory of the state, if he had always kept this distinction in sight.[3]

At least in Kant's case – that of Hegel is somewhat more obscure – there is a clear and respectable motive for this divorce between the idea of the general will and the empirical wants of citizens. Kant did not want the content of either morality or the principles of political right to be mortgaged to the messy details of human psychology. Rather, the content of both was to be fixed by an abstract consideration of what would be necessary for the co-existence of a plurality of individual wills. The contemplation of the conditions necessary for the agreement of those wills aims to get at what reason dictates, and what reason dictates is independent of the shortcomings that particular humans happen to have.

In the twentieth century, as we have seen, the most significant contribution to political philosophy in the English-speaking world, that of John Rawls in *A Theory of Justice*, has closely followed the Kantian lead of using the idea of a social contract and of the general will, as a pure idea of reason, separate from any actual willing that people might get up to. Rousseauian influence is plain both in Rawls's original position and in the idea of public reason that Rawls articulates in his later writings. Similarly, Jürgen Habermas's contractarian device, the 'ideal speech situation' is also of Rousseauian provenance, though, as with Rawls, its Kantian filtration ensures its divorce from actual people. In his writings on democracy, though, and in his critique of Rawls's work, Habermas has moved back in Rousseau's direction by insisting on the need for constitutional essentials to be the subject of real deliberations by real citizens.[4]

None of this is to say, of course, that philosophically, such idealising uses of the Rousseauian heritage are inappropriate. Not at all, the test of their appropriateness here is their fecundity in moral reflection. The point to make, though, is that this disembodied understanding of the general will was not Rousseau's own.

IS THE *SOCIAL CONTRACT* CONTRACTARIAN?

One final puzzle to address: is the *Social Contract*, despite its title, contractarian? Social contract theories such as those of Hobbes and Locke seek to ground individuals' reason to submit to the authority of the sovereign in the fact that they would have had reason to agree to the original contract such as each described. (The Hobbesian and Lockean stories are also complex and controversial, and this is an oversimplification, but I express it thus to draw a contrast with Rousseau.) Hobbesian and Lockean individuals within the state, differ from Rousseauian ones in that they retain the same psychology and human nature as the hypothetical contractors whose reasons for action are being appealed to by the theory. Rousseau's citizens, though, have, according to the pseudochronology of the *Social Contract* undergone a 'remarkable change' (1.8.1). The reasons that Rousseau's original contractors have for associating have to do with the preservation of their freedom and with the preservation of their lives. The reasons citizens within Rousseau's civil state have for continuing with their enterprise together may *include* the reasons the original associates had, but they go far beyond them. In particular, one of the types of freedom they have in the state, 'moral freedom', is a fruit of their association and could not be anticipated beforehand. The same goes for their feelings of shared identity and solidarity with their fellow citizens. Moreover, insofar as the *Social Contract* provides a solution to the problem of social coexistence for people whose *amour propre* has been awakened, it is a solution that they can come to value and appreciate only retrospectively – again, it could not figure among their original reasons for association. So while there may be a contractarian justification for the political association Rousseauian individuals end up in, it is not the justification that commends itself most strongly to them. If there is a contractarian justification – on Hobbesian or Lockean lines – for the Rousseauian state, it is one that is largely self-effacing.[5]

But in another, and perhaps more modern sense, the *Social Contract* remains a contractarian work. The state which it justifies is justified to the reason of each separate associate, and the reasons that each of them has for affirming their allegiance to it are genuinely good reasons, not ones of false consciousness. The state of the social contract enables citizens to live together with other social beings like themselves in a manner which allows each to pursue his ends consistent with a due respect for the right of other citizens to pursue *their* ends. This 'liberal' state of autonomous mutual coexistence, though, depends in turn on their building a common identity and civic culture of a kind of which liberals remain suspicious.

ROUSSEAU'S ENDURING IMPORTANCE

Rousseau's focus on the common or public interest and the need to intervene to protect it against private sectional interests, marks a very different emphasis in his work from the one we often find in the Anglo-American liberal tradition. Libertarians, for example, tend to see the world in terms of two relevant actors: the state and the individual, with the political task being to restrain the state's power over the individual. But people can become enslaved to private power too, even via contracts they have voluntarily engaged in. And the nominally public power can be captured by private corporate interests. Rousseau's importance lies in his trying to think through what is needed if individuals are to escape becoming subject to the private wills of other individuals. We may not be comfortable with all of his answers, but he squarely addresses faults in political culture and institutions that are plainly still with us and the *Social Contract* remains an indispensable resource in thinking about political power, legitimacy and freedom.

NOTES

1   In contemporary political philosophy we might point to the work of John Rawls as one prominent attempt to update the Rousseauian programme: Rawls values the liberties individuals enjoy but is sensitive to the way in which material inequalities among citizens can undermine the value of those liberties.

2   On Rousseau and Sièyes see Wokler, 'Ancient Postmodernism in the Philosophy of Rousseau', pp. 418–44. I take Robespierre's claim about the Committee of Public Safety from Mandle, 'Rousseauian Constructivism', p. 554 n. 19.

3   Hegel, *Hegel's Logic*, p. 228.

4   See, for example, Habermas, 'Reconciliation through the Public Use of Reason', pp. 109–31.

5   A possibility I explore in my, 'Self-Effacing Hobbesianism'. The phrase itself is first used by Joshua Cohen in his 'Reflections on Rousseau: Autonomy and Democracy'.

BIBLIOGRAPHY

Works by authors other than Rousseau are listed here. For details on cited works by Rousseau, see p. ix.

Aristotle. *Politics*, trans. Sir Ernest Barker (Oxford: Clarendon Press, 1948).

Bales, Kevin. 'The Social Psychology of Modern Slavery', *Scientific American*, April 2002.

Berlioz, Hector. *Memoirs*, trans. Ernest Newman (New York: Tudor Publishing Co., 1932).

Bertram, Christopher. 'Self-Effacing Hobbesianism', *Proceedings of the Aristotelian Society*, vol. XCIV (1994).

Bertram, Christopher. 'Language, Music and the Transparent Society in the *Essay on the Origin of Languages* and the *Social Contract*', forthcoming in *Studies in Voltaire and the Eighteenth Century*.

Boehm, Christopher. *Hierarchy in the Forest – the Evolution of Egalitarian Behaviour* (Cambridge, Mass.: Harvard University Press, 1999).

Cohen, Joshua. 'Reflections on Rousseau: Autonomy and Democracy', *Philosophy and Public Affairs*, vol. 16, no. 3 (1986), pp. 275–97.

Cohen, Joshua. 'The Natural Goodness of Humanity', in Andrews Reath ed. *Reclaiming the History of Ethics: Essays for John Rawls* (Cambridge: Cambridge University Press, 1997).

Cranston, Maurice. *Jean-Jacques: The Early Life and Work of Jean-Jacques Rousseau 1712–1754* (Harmondsworth: Penguin, 1983).

Cranston, Maurice. *The Noble Savage: Jean-Jacques Rousseau 1754–1762* (Harmondsworth: Penguin, 1991).

Cranston, Maurice. *The Solitary Self: Jean-Jacques Rousseau in Exile and Adversity* (Harmondsworth: Allen Lane, 1997).

Dent, N. J. H. *Rousseau* (Oxford: Blackwell, 1988).

Dent, N. J. H. *A Rousseau Dictionary* (Oxford: Blackwell, 1992).

Derathé, Robert. *Jean-Jacques Rousseau et La Science Politique de son Temps* (Paris: Vrin, 1950).

Diderot, Denis. *Political Writings*, eds Robert Wokler and John Hope Mason (Cambridge: Cambridge University Press, 1992).

Dworkin, Ronald. *Law's Empire* (Cambridge, Mass.: Harvard University Press, 1986).

Fralin, Richard. *Rousseau and Representation* (New York: Columbia University Press, 1978).

Françon, Marcel. 'Le Langage mathématique de Rousseau', in *Cahiers pour l'analyse* 8 (1970), pp. 85–8.

Gildin, Hilail. *Rousseau's Social Contract: The Design of the Argument* (Chicago, Ill.: University of Chicago Press, 1983).

Gourevitch, Victor. 'Recent Work on Rousseau', *Political Theory*, vol. 26, no. 4 (August 1998), pp. 536–56.

Grotius. *The Law of War and Peace*, trans. Louise R. Loomis (Roslyn, NY: Walter J. Black, 1949).

Habermas, Jürgen. 'Reconciliation through the Public Use of Reason: Remarks on Rawls' Political Liberalism', *Journal of Philosophy*, vol. 42, no. 2 (1995), pp. 109–31.

Halbwachs, Maurice. *Jean-Jacques Rousseau: Du Contrat Social* (Paris: Aubier, 1943).

Hegel, G. W. *Hegel's Logic*, 3rd edn, trans. William Wallace (Oxford: Clarendon Press, 1975).

Hobbes, Thomas. *De Cive*, in Thomas Hobbes, *Man and Citizen*, ed. Bernard Gert (Garden City, NY: Doubleday, 1972).

Hobbes, Thomas. *Leviathan*, ed. Richard Tuck (Cambridge: Cambridge University Press, 1991).

Hume, David. 'Of Commerce', in Stephen Copley and Andrew Edgar eds *Hume: Selected Essays* (Oxford: Oxford University Press, 1998).

Jones, W. T. 'Rousseau's General Will and the Problem of Consent', *Journal of the History of Philosophy*, vol. 25 (1987), pp. 105–30.

Kant, Immanuel. *Critique of Pure Reason*, trans. Norman Kemp-Smith (London: Macmillan, 1929).

Kant, Immanuel. *The Metaphysical Elements of Justice*, trans. John Ladd (New York: Macmillan, 1965).

Kant, Immanuel. 'On the Common Saying: "This May be True in Theory, but it does not Apply in Practice"', in Hans Reiss ed. *Kant: Political Writings* (Cambridge: Cambridge University Press, 1991), pp. 61–92.

Kaplan, Robert B. *Warrior Politics: Why Leadership Demands a Pagan Ethos* (New York: Random House, 2002).

Keohane, Nannerl. *Philosophy and the State in France: The Renaissance to the Enlightenment* (Princeton, N.J.: Princeton University Press, 1980).

Lemay, Edna Hindie. 'Rousseau et la peine de mort à l'Assemblée constituante', in *Études sur le* Contrat social/*Studies on the* Social Contract, *Pensée libre* no. 2 (1989), pp. 29–40.

Lewis, C. S. 'The Humanitarian Theory of Punishment', in Walter Hooper ed. *God in the Dock* (Grand Rapids, Mich.: William B. Eerdmans, 1970).

Locke, John. *Two Treatises of Government*, ed. Peter Laslett (Cambridge: Cambridge University Press, 1988).

Locke, John. *A Letter Concerning Toleration*, eds John Horton and Susan Mendus (London: Routledge, 1991).

Machiavelli, Niccolao. *The Prince and the Discourses*, with an introduction by Max Lerner (New York: The Modern Library, 1950).

Madison, James and Hamilton, Alexander. *The Federalist Papers*, ed. Isaac Kramnick (London: Penguin, 1987).

Mandle, Jon. 'Rousseauian Constructivism', *Journal of the History of Philosophy*, vol. 35, no. 4 (October 1997), pp. 545–62.

Marini, Frank. 'Popular Sovereignty but Representative Government: The Other Rousseau', *Midwest Journal of Political Science*, vol. 11, no. 4 (November 1967), pp. 451–70.

Marx, Karl. 'The Eighteenth Brumaire of Louis Bonaparte', in David Fernbach ed. *Surveys from Exile* (Harmondsworth: Penguin, 1973).

Masters, Roger D. *The Political Philosophy of Rousseau* (Princeton, N.J.: Princeton University Press, 1968).

Masters, Roger D. *The Nature of Politics* (New Haven, Conn.: Yale University Press, 1989).

McNeill, William H. *Keeping Together in Time: Dance and Drill in Human History* (Cambridge, Mass.: Harvard University Press, 1995).

Melzer, Arthur M. *The Natural Goodness of Humanity: On the System of Rousseau's Thought* (Chicago, Ill.: University of Chicago Press, 1990).

Mill, John Stuart. *'On Liberty' and Other Writings*, ed. Stefan Collini (Cambridge: Cambridge University Press, 1989).

Montesquieu, Baron de. *The Spirit of the Laws*, trans. Thomas Nugent (New York: Hafner Press, 1949).

Montesquieu, Baron de. *Persian Letters*, trans. C. J. Betts (Harmondsworth: Penguin, 1973), p. 191.

Neuhouser, Frederick. 'Freedom, Dependence, and the General Will', *Philosophical Review*, vol. 102, no. 3 (1993), pp. 363–95.

O' Hagan, Timothy. *Rousseau* (London: Routledge, 1999).

Paul, Charles B. 'Music and Ideology: Rameau, Rousseau and 1789', *Journal of the History of Ideas*, vol. 32, no. 3 (July–September 1971), pp. 395–410.

Plato. *Complete Works*, ed. John M. Cooper, various translators (Indianapolis, Ind.: Hackett, 1997).

Rawls, John. *A Theory of Justice* (Cambridge, Mass.: Harvard University Press, 1971).

Raz, Joseph. *The Morality of Freedom* (Oxford: Oxford University Press, 1986).

Riley, Patrick. *The General Will Before Rousseau* (Princeton, N.J.: Princeton University Press, 1986).

Roosevelt, Grace G. *Reading Rousseau in the Nuclear Age* (Philadelphia, Pa.: Temple University Press, 1990).

Rosenblatt, Helena. *Rousseau and Geneva: From the First Discourse to the Social Contract 1749–1762* (Cambridge: Cambridge University Press, 1997).

Roth, Philip. *The Professor of Desire* (New York: Farrar, Straus and Giroux, 1977).

Scott, James C. *Domination and the Arts of Resistance* (New Haven, Conn.: Yale University Press, 1990).

Scott, John T. 'Politics as the Imitation of the Divine in Rousseau's *Social Contract*', *Polity* 26 (Summer 1994), pp. 473–501.

Scott, John T. 'Rousseau and the Melodious Language of Freedom', *The Journal of Politics*, vol. 59, no. 3 (August 1997).

Shklar, Judith N. *Men and Citizens*, 2nd edition (Cambridge: Cambridge University Press, 1985).

Simmons, A. John. *Moral Principles and Political Obligations* (Princeton, N.J.: Princeton University Press, 1981).

Smith, Michael. *The Moral Problem* (Oxford: Blackwell, 1994).

Sober, Elliott. *The Nature of Selection: Evolutionary Theory in Philosophical Focus* (Cambridge, Mass.: MIT Press, 1984).

Spinoza, Benedict. *A Political Treatise*, in *A Theologico-Political Treatise and a Political Treatise*, translated with an introduction by R. H. M. Elwes, with a Bibliographical Note by Francesco Cordasco (New York: Dover Publications, 1951).

Sreenivasan, Gopal. 'What is the General Will?', *Philosophical Review*, vol. 109, no. 4 (2000), pp. 545–81.

Starobinski, Jean. *Jean-Jacques Rousseau: Le Transparence et L'Obstacle* (Paris: Gallimard, 1976).

Steiner, Hillel. *An Essay on Rights* (Oxford: Blackwell, 1994).

Strawson, P. F. 'Freedom and Resentment', in his *Studies in the Philosophy of Thought and Action* (Oxford: Oxford University Press, 1968).

Strong, Tracy B. *Jean-Jacques Rousseau: The Politics of the Ordinary* (Thousand Oaks, Ca.: Sage, 1994).

Taylor, Michael. *Community, Anarchy and Liberty* (Cambridge: Cambridge University Press, 1982).

Trachtenberg, Zev M. *Making Citizens: Rousseau's Political Theory of Culture* (London: Routledge, 1993).

Williams, David ed. *The Enlightenment* (Cambridge: Cambridge University Press, 1999).

Wokler, Robert. 'Perfectible apes in decadent cultures: Rousseau's anthropology revisited', *Daedalus*, vol. 107, no. 3 (1978), pp. 107–34.

Wokler, Robert. 'The Enlightenment: The Nation-State and the Primal Patricide of Modernity', in Norman Geras and Robert Wokler eds *The Enlightenment and Modernity* (London: Macmillan, 2000).

Wokler, Robert. 'Ancient Postmodernism in the Philosophy of Rousseau', in Patrick Riley ed. *The Cambridge Companion to Rousseau* (Cambridge: Cambridge University Press, 2001), pp. 418–44.

Wolff, Robert Paul. *In Defense of Anarchism* (New York: HarperCollins, 1970).

INDEX